THE ORDERING OF LOVE

THE ORDERING OF LOVE

The New and
Collected Poems of

Foreword by Sarah Arthur
Reader's Guide by Lindsay Lackey

CONVERGENT

New York

2020 Convergent Books Trade Paperback Edition

Copyright © 2005 by Crosswicks, Ltd.
Foreword copyright © 2020 by Penguin Random House LLC
Reader's Guide copyright © 2020 by Penguin Random House LLC

Library of Congress Cataloging-in-Publication Data
L'Engle, Madeleine.
The ordering of love : the new and collected poems of Madeleine
    L'Engle.—1st ed.
p. cm.
Includes bibliographical references and indexes.
I. Title.
PS3523.E55O74 2005
811'.54—dc22

ISBN 978-0-307-73183-8
Ebook ISBN 978-0-307-55145-0

Printed in the United States of America on acid-free paper

convergentbooks.com

9 8 7 6 5 4

Contents

FROM *THE WEATHER OF THE HEART* (1978)

FROM *A CRY LIKE A BELL* (1987)

UNCOLLECTED POEMS (CIRCA 1966)

UNCOLLECTED POEMS (CIRCA 1998)

Foreword

Madeleine L'Engle's first book of poetry, *Lines Scribbled on an Envelope,* was published by Farrar, Straus & Giroux in 1969. It's a curious thing, because what she should've been working on—as any publisher would have hoped—was the sequel, or numerous sequels, to her children's sci-fi novel *A Wrinkle in Time,* which had won the Newbery Award in 1963.

It's not that she wasn't writing. If anything, the six years between her Newbery and her poetry collection were tremendously prolific, yielding multiple books in the Austin Family Chronicles, a novel for grown-ups titled *The Love Letters,* and even a biblically inspired morality play, *The Journey with Jonah.* But the sequel to *A Wrinkle in Time* wouldn't appear until *A Wind in the Door* in 1973, with other sequels spread out over the next two decades.

Why the delay? Why the almost obstinate refusal to fulfill the expectations of fans and the publishing world? Because L'Engle had her own ideas about the creative process. She wasn't there to serve the market; she was there to "serve the work." As she later described in her landmark treatise on faith and art, *Walking on Water* (1980), "If the work comes to the artist and says, 'Here I am, serve me,' then the job of the artist, great or small, is to serve." And so it was with her poetry.

By publishing her poetry, her editor wasn't merely indulging a favored author. L'Engle wrote good poetry. Indeed, if she'd never written anything else, an Internet search about her today might yield results beginning with "Madeleine L'Engle was a twentieth-century American poet." Her life as a poet started in childhood, in a lonely New York apartment while her parents were busy in the literary-arts scene of the Roaring Twenties. Books were some of her only companions. She read whatever she could find—fairy tales, poetry, the Bible—and when she ran out of things to read, she wrote.

Friendless, overlooked, and underappreciated by her teachers, she gave up on trying to please everyone and instead wrote poetry and stories when she should've been doing homework. When one of her poems anonymously won a fifth-grade poetry prize and L'Engle was revealed as the author, her teacher assumed the underachieving child must've plagiarized it. As L'Engle describes in the first of her memoiresque Crosswicks Journals, *A Circle of Quiet,* her mother gathered Madeleine's writing from home to prove that her daughter most definitely could've written a prize-winning poem.

This early story speaks volumes about the person L'Engle would become—not only about her writing, but also about her character: her quirkiness, her tenacity, her nonconformity. When publishers tried to box her in to one audience or genre for a given book, she stubbornly refused to comply ("It's for *people*! Don't *people* read books?"). Like British author C. S. Lewis (*The Chronicles of Narnia, The Screwtape Letters*), she wrote in a formidable range of genres, for a formidable range of readers—everything from mainstream fiction, drama, and memoir with New York publishing houses to spiritual nonfiction, midrash-like biblical commentary, and poetry with smaller religious presses. As her granddaughter and literary executor,

Charlotte Jones Voiklis, once playfully exclaimed to me, "She was a witch!" Madeleine's literary dexterity was a kind of shape-shifting: whatever form she needed, she took.

Yet Madeleine L'Engle was disciplined as well: from childhood she knew the rules of grammar and of rhyme and meter (even if her spelling was British rather than American), and she followed them. More important, she understood early on that the work itself requires a kind of dogged servitude, that you show up and serve it, whether you feel like it—or whether anyone appreciates it—or not.

She likened this vocational discipline to practicing daily piano scales or a Bach fugue: your fingers learn the form while your brain and imagination engage in their own kind of muscle memory. It's also the posture she took toward spiritual practices such as prayer. On a given day you may not feel like praying, but daily participation in that ritual builds spiritual muscle. As her good friend Barbara Braver told Leonard Marcus in his collection of interviews *Listening for Madeleine*, "[Madeleine] had the structure, and within that there would be distractions and surprises: welcome and often stretching, and full of grace."

When in *A Wrinkle in Time* Mrs Whatsit likens life to a sonnet—as it has a prescribed structure but what you say is up to you—she's not spouting just any old metaphor. For L'Engle, the sonnet was both a recurring metaphor as well as a personal discipline; it became her poetic specialty. One could argue that the more constraints the literary form puts on the writer, the more the writer must serve the work, must get herself out of the way. This means that a poetic form such as a sonnet requires a tremendous amount of humility, for the writer can only say what the form allows—no more, no less. There's no room for indulging one's moods by scribbling one's stream of consciousness. For a sonnet to say something with fluid freshness, in the writer's unique voice, requires tremendous skill; otherwise it risks devolving into stilted, impersonal verse.

Somehow within that form Madeleine L'Engle not only exercised masterful technique but also the humility to be confessional. Take, for example, the poem cycle "To a Long-Loved Love," where we perhaps learn more about the nature of her marriage to actor Hugh Franklin than in her memoiresque *Two-Part Invention: The Story of a Marriage* (1988). At times her nonfiction betrays the controlling hand of the inveterate storyteller while her poetry, by contrast, is almost indistinguishable in its humility from prayer—at times, it *is* prayer.

Not long after her first poetry collection went out of print, it got the attention of the small religious press Harold Shaw Publishers, thanks to L'Engle's chance meeting in the early 1970s with poet and editor Luci Shaw, who would become her lifelong friend. Shaw became the editor and publisher of L'Engle's poetry, including *The Weather of the Heart* (1978), *A Cry Like a Bell* (1987), and her collected poetry, *The Ordering of Love* (2005). With Barbara Braver, who stayed with L'Engle in the 1990s while commuting to work in NYC, L'Engle and Shaw spent many hours together, including a trip in 1995 to Iona and Lindisfarne, where Braver recalls the three of them writing poetry in an old cemetery. L'Engle was then in her late 70s, still prolific, still showing up for the work that needed to be written.

Writing became more elusive for L'Engle after the death of her son Bion in 1999 to end-stage alcoholism—a disease which she never acknowledged and a tragedy from which she never recovered. *The Ordering of Love* first came out two years before her death in 2007; even now, with this new edition, it's poignant to realize there will be no new poems here. The last lines of the sonnet that was Madeleine L'Engle's life have already been written, but within the form there is still a liveliness, a humility, a prayerful and powerful portrait of a writer who served her work, and served it well. May we strive to do the same.

—Sarah Arthur

THE ORDERING OF LOVE

FROM *LINES*

SCRIBBLED ON AN

ENVELOPE

(1969)

To a Long-Loved Love

(i)

We, who have seen the new moon grow old together,
Who have seen winter rime the fields and stones
As though it would claim earth and water forever,
We who have known the touch of flesh and the shape of
      bones
Know the old moon stretching its shadows across a
      whitened field
More beautiful than spring with all its spate of blooms;
What passion knowledge of tried flesh still yields,
What joy and comfort these familiar rooms.

(ii)

In the moonless, lampless dark now of this bed
My body knows each line and curve of yours;
My fingers know the shape of limb and head:
As pure as mathematics ecstasy endures.
Blinded by night and love we share our passion,
Certain of burning flesh, of living bone:
So feels the sculptor in the moment of creation
Moving his hands across the uncut stone.

(iii)

I know why a star gives light
Shining quietly in the night;
Arithmetic helps me unravel
The hours and years this light must travel
To penetrate our atmosphere.
I can count the craters on the moon

With telescopes to make them clear.
With delicate instruments I can measure
The secrets of barometric pressure.

And therefore I find it inexpressibly queer
That with my own soul I am out of tune,
And that I have not stumbled on the art
Of forecasting the weather of the heart.

The Mermaid

My father gives me everything
I ask for. Don't you envy me?
I swim faster than a bird can wing.
Sea gulls cannot catch me: see?
Who else has hair of silk sea green?
Or silver scales, shining, alive?
My father's king (there is no queen).
I can dive full fathom five.

You wonder why I never cry?
Why mermaids have no need for tears?
Upon my sea-salt rock I lie
And play with time and laugh at years
And send my song along the air
And sing my call to passing ships,
And there is nothing quite so fair
As the cold touch of dead men's lips.

My father gives me everything,
Gold and frankincense and mer—
Boys for my sport. I lie and sing.
A sailor shouts, "Don't look at her!"
I lie upon my sea-swept stone
And wait. The sailor hears and cries.
More bleached white bones to call my own
And his salt tears before he dies.

My father gives me everything.

That's just sea water in my eyes.

Lines Scribbled on an Envelope While Riding the 104 Broadway Bus:

There is too much pain
I cannot understand
I cannot pray

I cannot pray for all the little ones with bellies bloated by
    starvation in India;
for all the angry Africans striving to be separate in a world
    struggling for wholeness;
for all the young Chinese men and women taught that
    hatred and killing are good and compassion evil;
or even all the frightened people in my own city looking
    for truth in pot or acid.

Here I am
and the ugly man with beery breath beside me reminds
    me that it is not my prayers that waken your
    concern, my Lord;
my prayers, my intercessions are not to ask for your love
for all your lost and lonely ones,
your sick and sinning souls,
but mine, my love, my acceptance of your love.
Your love for the woman sticking her umbrella and her
    expensive
parcels into my ribs and snarling, "Why don't you watch
    where you're going?"

Your love for the long-haired, gum-chewing boy who
        shoves the old lady aside to grab a seat,
Your love for me, too, too tired to look with love,
too tired to look at Love, at you, in every person on the
        bus.
Expand my love, Lord, so I can help to bear the pain,
help your love move my love into the tired prostitute with
        false eyelashes and bunioned feet,
the corrupt policeman with his hand open for graft,
the addict, the derelict, the woman in the mink coat and
        discontented mouth,
the high school girl with heavy books and frightened eyes.

Help me through these scandalous particulars
to understand
your love.

Help me to pray.

Shout Joy!

O sing unto God
and sing praises unto his Name
magnify him that rideth upon the heavens
praise him in his Name
Jah!
shout it
cry it aloud upon the wind
take the tail of his steed
and fling across the sky
in his wild wake
Jah!
he cannot be caught
he cannot be fled
he cannot be known
nor his knowledge escaped
the light of his Name
blinds the brilliance of stars
Jah!
catch the falling dragon
ride between his flailing wings
leap between the jaws of the lion
grasp the horn of the unicorn
calling with mighty voice
Jah!
caught in star flame
whipped by comet lash
rejoice before him
cry above the voices of the cherubim
shout alongside the seraphim

Jah!
bellow joy behind kings
scattered by the quaking of his hills
fleeing before his fire
rush like snow through his thunderous flame
crying with gladness
adoration of his Name
God is Lord
Jah!

"Body, the black horse and the white"

Body, the black horse and the white,
Who bears me through the day and night,
How shall I ride when you are gone?
Without my steed am I undone?
Black horse and white, O wingèd horse,
Sinister, dextrous, holding course,
O wingèd horse with single horn,
O Pegasus, O unicorn,
Body my body, when you're in grave
Will I have any soul to save?
Body, our journey's just begun,
And rider, ridden, are only one.
How can I see your rank corruption
Except as journey's interruption?
Where am I going? How can I travel
Without my body? Truth: unravel:
Body, as dark as starless night,
Tell me, where comes the blinding light?
Body it is whose ears have heard
The thunder crashing of the Word.
The lightning flash reveals what face?
Where are we going? To what place?
How shall I ride when you are done?
How shall I once again be one?

Medusa

(Because she had angered the gods, Medusa was the only one of the Gorgons who was not immortal.)

I, of all Gorgons, I, alone, must die.
Since death must come to me I carry death
At all times in my face, my bitter eye.
If every breath I draw is mortal breath
Leading irrevocably to my end
I'll give stone death to all who see my face,
My span of life resentfully will spend
Denying life: revenge for my disgrace.
I, who should be immortal, have been shamed,
But cloak my shame in serpent hissing pride.
Immortal privilege denied, self maimed,
Only this arrogance can fury hide.
Think you I like the snakes upon my head?
My only pleasure is in luring men
To look, to turn to granite, silent, dead.
Then what's their use? The worst is when
Gods look on me and laugh. But look you, mortal,
I'll blast you through death's icy portal.
Thus in your death my own have I delayed.
Not god, not human—Medusa is afraid.

Lines After Sir Thomas Browne

If thou couldst empty self of selfishness
And then with love reach out in wide embrace
Then might God come this purer self to bless;
So might thou feel the wisdom of His Grace,
And see, thereby, the radiance of His face.

But selfishness turns inwards, miry, black,
Refuses stars, sees only clouded night,
Too full, too dark, cannot confess a lack,
Turns from God's face, blest, holy, bright,
Is blinded by the presence of the Light.

The Unicorn

(The unicorn is an untamed beast who always eludes the pursuit of hunters—unless he sees a young virgin. Then he will lie down with his head in her lap and can be easily taken.)

I am feral, free, untame,
So wild I do not have a name.
One-horn, you say? That's what I am,
But who I am I cannot tell,
For I am only that I am.
My neigh is like a forest knell
And you will never know the rapture
Of my swift flight, eluding capture.

I am not young, nor grow I old.
My heart beats softly, quiet, cold,
Is moved by no one: woman, man.
My veins are ice.
              Wait!
                   Who goes there?
My heart stopped for a frightened span.
What is this tension in the air?
Oh, girl, not woman, more than child,
Which of us two is the more wild?

So quietly you sit and wait.
Wait: why? For whom? Am I too late?
I do not know what joy this is.

The blood runs in me like the sap.
I come to you in freedom. This
Is bliss, my head upon your lap.
Nothing will ever be the same.
Someone: tell me! What's my name?

Abraham's Child

Towards afternoon the train pulled in to the station.
The light came grey and cold through the dirty glass of
    the terminal roof,
and passengers waiting on the platform blew upon their
    hands and stamped their feet
and their breath came out like smoke.
In the comfortable compartment I leaned back against the
    red plush of the seat
and looked out the window. All the signs were in a
    language I could not read.
I got out my passport and held it, waiting in readiness.
My papers were in order and the train was warm.
The conductor slid open the door to the compartment and
    said to me,
"This is your last stop on this train. You will have to get
    out."
I held out my passport, "No, no, my journey's barely half
    over,"
and I told him the cities through which the train was
    going to pass.
He handed me back my passport and said again, "You will
    have to get out,"
and he took me by the arms and led me from the coach.
His hands were so strong my arms cried out in pain. On
    the platform it was cold.
"But I don't know where I am!" I cried, "or where I am
    going."
"Follow me," he said. "I have been sent to show you."

Through the glass of the station roof I could see the sun
     was going down
and a horror of great darkness fell upon me.
"Come," the conductor said. "This is the way you are
     to go,"
and he led me past the passengers waiting on the platform
and past the foreign signs and a burning lamp in this land
where I was a stranger. He led me to a train with no lights
     and broken windows
and a pale wisp of smoke lifting from a rusty engine, and
     said,
"Get in. This is your train."
I fell upon my face and laughed and said, "But this train
     isn't going anywhere,"
and he said, "You may sit down," and I sat on a wooden
     bench
and he put my satchel on the rack over my head.
"Are you ready for the journey?" he asked me. "I must
     have your passport."
I gave it to him. "Where are we going?" I asked. The train
     was cold.
"The way will be shown," he said, and closed the
     compartment door.
I heard a puff of steam. The old engine began to pull the
     dark car
and we ventured out into the night.

The Promise

You promised
well, actually you didn't promise very much, did you?
but that little is enough
is more than enough.
We fail you
over and over again
but you promised to be faithful to us
not to let us fail
beyond your forgiveness of our failure.
In our common temptation
you promised
we would not be tempted more than we are able
you promised not to lead us into temptation
beyond our frail strength
and you
yourself
are our refuge in temptation
our escape from the pit
and that is enough
so that we can bear
more than we thought we could bear
of loneliness, nothingness, otherness,
sin, silliness, sadness.
For thine is the kingdom and the other great fors:
forbearance, forgiveness,
fortitude,
forever:
this is what you promised
it is enough
it is everything.

Primate

I went into a building called a church.
A lot of monkeys sat in all the pews
and at the altar there were other monkeys
dressed in fancy clothes.
Everybody was very busy. The monkeys kept kneeling
and crossing themselves and some of them
kept looking around to see that they did everything
the other monkeys did, and maybe a little more.
They went up to the altar and their palms were pressed
       together
so that they looked very holy and they ate and drank
and the monkeys at the altar said some gibberish
and the air rang with the monkery and mockery
of words repeated until the fragment of an echo
was all that could be heard of what had once been said.

Afterwards the monkeys all shook hands and showed their
       teeth
and drank coffee to break their pious fast
and some scratched each other's backs and others
scratched at monkeys who weren't there
and all the monkeys looked around to see
if they were talking to the most important monkeys
so nobody listened to anybody else.

I went home and looked into the mirror
and raised a prehensile finger to scratch behind
my simian ear. Oh, God. O God:
where is your image?

Testament

O God
I will do thy will.
I will
to do thy will.

How can my will
will to do thy will?
If I will
to know thy will
then I fall on my own will.
How can I will
to love or to obey?
My very willing bars the way.
Willingness becomes self-will.

O God
if thou will
turn my will to thy will
if thou will
tell me thy will
it will
be in spite of
not because of
my will.

Help me to lose my will.
Each day
let my will die
so will I

be born.
New born will I live
willingly   lovingly
and will
will be no more

will be thine
O God
if thou will.

People in Glass Houses

I build my house of shining glass
of crystal
prisms
light, clear,
delicate.
The wind blows
Sets my rooms to singing.
The sun's bright rays
are not held back
but pour
their radiance through the rooms
in sparkles of delight.

And what, you ask, of rain
that leaves blurred muddy streaks
across translucent purity?
What, you ask,
of the throwers of stones?

Glass shatters,
breaks,
sharp fragments pierce my flesh,
darken with blood.
The wind tinkles brittle splinters
of shivered crystal.
The stones crash through.

But never mind.
My house

My lovely shining
fragile broken house
is filled with flowers
and founded on a rock.

The Phoenix

(There are many and varying legends about the beautiful gold and scarlet bird, the Phoenix. One is that he returns to Heliopolis every five hundred years, and that he is born again out of his own ashes.)

Vulnerability is my only armour.
I, the colour of fire, of blazing sun,
A blare of yellow and gold, and not a murmur
Of feathers of grey or brown, how can I run

From friend or foe? How could I ever hide?
I shall fly freely across the threatening sky
And I shall sing. Call it, if you like, pride.
I call it joy. Perhaps it's love. My eye

Is moist with all that brings it such delight.
I love this city thronging with the day,
And all the shadows crowding in the night.
Five hundred years since I have been this way,

O city full of children, wise men, fools,
Laughter and love, and hatred, scheming, murder,
Starvation among gluttons, brothels, schools;
I fly above the city and bring order

Out of this chaos. O small hungry child
Put up your bow, put down the piercing arrow
So that your hands may still be undefiled.
All through the city I must cleanse and harrow.

Aaaaagh! I am wounded by a hunter's spear.
Against the earth my dying body crashes.
The child who did not shoot me wails in fear.
Hot on my golden feathers swift blood gushes.

Blood stains the faggots of the funeral pyre.
My eyes grow dim among the flames' wild flashes.
The child is weeping still; the flames burn higher.
Hush. I shall be born from these dead ashes.

Moses

Come.
　　When?
Now. This way. I will guide you.
　　Wait! Not so fast.
Hurry. You. I said you.
　　Who am I?
Certainly I will be with thee.
　　Is nothing, then, what it is? I had rather the rod had
　　　　stayed
　　a rod and not become a serpent.
Come. Quickly. While the blast of my breath opens the sea.
　　Stop. I'm thirsty.
Drink water from this rock.
　　But the rock moves on before us.
Go with it and drink.
　　I'm tired. Can't you stop for a while?
You have already tarried too long.
　　But if I am to follow you I must know your name.
I will be that I will be.
　　You have set the mountain on fire.
Come. Climb.
　　I will be lost in the terror of your cloud.
You are stiff-necked and of a stiff-necked people.
　　YOUR people, Lord,
Indubitably.
　　Your wrath waxes hot. I burn.
Thus to become great.
　　Show me then thy glory.

No man may see my face and live. But I will cover you
    with my hand while I pass by.
  My people turn away and cry because the skin of my
    face shines.
Did you not expect this?
  I cannot enter the tent of the congregation because your
    cloud covers it and your glory fills the tabernacle.
    Look. It moves before us again. Can you not stay still?
Come. Follow.
  But this river is death. The waters are dark and deep.
Swim.
  Now will I see your face? Where are you taking me
    now?
Up the mountain with me before I die.
  But death
bursts into light.
  Then death is
what it will be.
  These men: they want to keep us here in three
    tabernacles. But the cloud moves. The water springs
    from a rock that journeys on.
You are contained in me.
  But how can we contain you in ark or tabernacle or
You cannot.
  Where, then?
In your heart. Come.
  Still?
I will be with thee.
  Who am I?
You are that I will be. Come.

From St. Luke's Hospital (1)

Pain is a bubble in the strange, stretched skin of time,
Not time itself, it presses harshly outside familiar
  chronology
Yet is surrounded by time, trapped far from the bliss of
  eternity.

But within this austere emptiness filled only by the
  anguished stab,
Eternity's touch ministers. Listen in this music-bereft hole:
His voice comes even here. There is no place or non-place
  left without his Word.

Sometimes to listen is part of the pain, is pulling the hurt
  through the dark
Not by one's own strength, but his. The cry for help is
  heard
Though it is hard to hear the hearing. Pain is borne by the
  bearing of the Word.

Passion Play

It is
again
the actor's nightmare
the recurring dream:
I am waiting in the wings
and I don't know my lines:
not only that,
I don't even know what rôle I am supposed to act
or what the play is about.
It's a large cast, and evidently a costume play
but I can't figure out the period:
there seem to be costumes from all centuries.
The curtain is up and the audience attentive
in the darkness
and I don't know any of my cues:
how can I tell when to make my entrance?
Everybody else is terribly busy, and people are saying
different lines simultaneously
so I really can't get the gist of the play.
There is one actor who moves quietly
instead of milling about
as though he,
of all the company,
understands the script
and has learned his lines and actions.
Perhaps if I go on stage and follow him . . .

But now everybody is after him;
they're all surrounding him

and shouting
they have him down on the stage
and the ground cloth is dusty and dirty

this isn't a proper play at all

the audience is clapping and shouting

and he lies there on the stage
his arms spread out

what are they doing?
they have a hammer and nails

wait

this is supposed to be a play
you're not supposed to hurt the actors
you're not supposed to kill the lead
where is the author?

stop them   somebody   stop them

where is the director?
where is the producer?

let me wake up
I don't want it to be real

it's just a play
people aren't like that

are we?

For Dana: 4th November

The end of the year is here. We are at a new beginning.
A birth has come, and we reenact
At its remembrance the extraordinary fact
Of our unique, incomprehensible being.

The new year has started, for moving and growing.
The child's laugh within and through the adult's tears,
In joy and incomprehension at the singing years
Pushes us into fresh life, new knowing.

Here at the end of the year comes the year's springing.
The falling and melting snow meet in the stream
That flows with living waters and cleanses the dream.
The reed bends and endures and sees the dove's winging.

Move into the year and the new time's turning
Open and vulnerable and loving and steady.
The stars are aflame; creation is ready.
The day is at hand: the bright sun burns.

The Roc

(The roc is a fabulous bird of Arabia, so huge it can carry several large beasts at a time to take home to feed its young.)

Hushabye, darlings, mama'll get dinner
So sweet little fledglings won't get any thinner.
    Rockabye, rocklings, roc, roc, roc a bye.

Spiders bring squiggly worms, small as your eyelash.
Salmon catch minnows, quick as a fly flash.
    Hairy red spiders give spiderlets lice.
    Cats bring their kittens home little grey mice.
Dogs bring their puppy dogs scraps from the table.
Howling hyenas steal what they are able.
    Rockabye, rocklings, roc, roc, roc a bye.

Monkeys to monklings say, "Breakfast, mañana,
Here, catch a coconut, peel a banana."
    Rhinoceros calves eat ostriches' eggs.
    Lion cubs squabble o'er antelope legs.
Mama and papa ahunting will go
O'er valleys of diamonds and moonscapes of snow.
    Rockabye, rocklings, roc, roc, roc a bye.

Ah, now I see them, look, rocklings, my word!
I'll bring you dinner right out of that herd.
    Pachyderms flee at the sight of a flock
    Of us terrible-taloned and talented roc,
But the only meal of suitable elegance
For a flock of young roc is a handful of elephants.
    Rockabye, rocklings, roc, roc, roc a bye.

Instruments (1)

The sky is strung with glory.
Light threads from star to star
from sun to sun
a living harp.
I rejoice, I sing, I leap upwards to play.
The music is in light.
My fingers pluck the vibrant strings;
the notes pulse, throb, in exultant harmony;
I beat my wings against the strands
that reach across the galaxies
I play

NO

It is not I who play
it is the music
the music plays itself
is played
plays me
small part of an innumerable
unnumberable
orchestra.
I am flung from note to note
impaled on melody
my wings are caught on throbbing filaments of light
the wild cords cut my pinions
my arms are stretched
are bound by ropes of counterpoint
I am cross-eagled on the singing that is strung

from pulsing star
to flaming sun
to

I burn in a blaze of song.

Instruments (2)

Hold me against the dark: I am afraid.
Circle me with your arms. I am made
So tiny and my atoms so unstable
That at any moment I may explode. I am unable
To contain myself in unity. My outlines shiver
With the shock of living. I endeavor
To hold the *I* as one only for the cloud
Of which I am a fragment, yet to which I'm vowed
To be responsible. Its light against my face
Reveals the witness of the stars, each in its place
Singing, each compassed by the rest,
The many joined to one, the mightiest to the least.
It is so great a thing to be an infinitesimal part
Of this immeasurable orchestra the music bursts the
        heart,
And from this tiny plosion all the fragments join:
Joy orders the disunity until the song is one.

The Baby in the Bath

Throw out the bath water.
Never mind the baby.
The water's dark and dirty
and if we toss it maybe
we'll learn to come to terms
with the viruses and germs
that are thinning out our ranks.

Throw out the bath water
never mind the baby
I think he's dead already;
at least he's been forgotten.
The water's rank and rotten
and you won't get any thanks
if you rock the sinking boat
so steady, lads, steady
if you hope to keep afloat

throw out the bath water.
Who ever is the baby?
He's nothing but a little lamb
who thinks he is and that I am.
Catch him, catch him if you're able,
serve him up upon the table,
catch and kill the little lamb,
garnish him and make him nice:
he'll do for a sacrifice.

Throw out the bath water.
Who is this tiny baby?
Just an infant, meek and mild,
just a feeble, human child,
dying quickly, if not dead:
he won't turn your stones to bread
(serve the lamb. We must be fed).
Moving surely through the gloom
on the path from womb to tomb
this babe can't help so throw him out
otherwise he'll waken doubt.

Throw out the bath water
never mind the baby
throw the water   watch it flood
in the mingling of the blood

throw out the bath water
who is this tiny baby?
nothing but   run for your life!

the babe is sharpening the knife
his army crashes through the sea
with angry banners. Run, oh, flee,
the trumpet blasts its brilliant notes
blown by wild and heavenly hosts
the red bath water's closing tide
will swallow all who do not hide

throw out the bath water
who is this tiny baby?

The Lord strong and mighty
even the Lord mighty in battle

run from the bath water
the Lord's alarum is sounded
run from the great avenging power
O circled, cornered, utterly surrounded
there is no place to hide or cower

throw out the
run
the king of glory's coming in
who is this
even the Lord of hosts
He is the tiny baby.

The Sea Monster

Boy! little boy!

You're going to board that ship? You dare?
To go beyond the sight of land?
They've warned you, boy? If not, beware
Of me. Beware of leaving sand

For sea. Beware of that sharp ledge
That marks the boundary of the world.
If your ship topples off the edge
I'm waiting there, my coils uncurled,

My tails athrash, my eyes afire,
My head wreathed in a flashing nimbus.
            What?
How dare you say that I'm a liar?
How dare you say that word: Columbus!

How dare your ship sail and not drop
When it encounters the horizon?
I wait forever for the plop
Of falling ships; I keep my eyes on

The line where sea stops at the sky,
But nothing falls: the sailing ship
Goes round and round and round and round,
A circumnavigating trip.

For land and sea are charted now;
None think of me; I am not missed.
And none can even tell you how
I talk when I do not exist.

If this round world were only square,
If this curved earth were only flat,
You'd find that I'd be waiting there,
A monster to be frightened at.

We Make Bold to Say . . .

When I was very little my father
used to toss me up in the air
and I would laugh and crow with delight
knowing that his outstretched arms
were there to receive me, that he would
never let me fall.

You have thrown me up into the coldness
beyond the galaxies. Your wild wind
blows me. Where are your hands
to catch me as I fall?

When I was very little my father
would sometimes come sit with me
at tea time. We had a game. Carefully
I would eat my egg out of its shell
and then put the shell, upside down, back
in the egg cup, and he, ferocious, would
say, "Eat your egg at once!" and together
we would open it and laugh in joy
at the empty shell.

Why has the egg turned to a
scorpion in my hand?

When I was very little my father
took me to watch the fishermen
pull in their nets leaping with silver

and he told me stories of whales and other
great fish and of ships and storms and of those
who were fishers of men.

Why is the serpent allowed to continue
spitting seductive poison in my ear?

When I was very little my father
would sometimes come in the splendor
of his white tie and tails to say me good-night
and he would let me hold the silkiness
of his top hat. He had one that
opened and shut with a sound like a shot
and this was laughter and joy, and when he left
there was always a crack of light
to shine through the bedroom door.

O father of all fathers
who takes from me the strength of words
and the comfort of images
I am alone in the dark and afraid.

The Birth of Love

To learn to love
is to be stripped of all love
until you are wholly without love
because
until you have gone
naked and afraid
into this cold dark place
where all love is taken from you
you will not know
that you are wholly within love.

Fire by Fire

My son goes down in the orchard to incinerate
Burning the day's trash, the accumulation
Of old letters, empty toilet-paper rolls, a paper plate,
Marketing lists, discarded manuscript, on occasion
Used cartons of bird seed, dog biscuit. The fire
Rises and sinks; he stirs the ashes till the flames expire.

Burn, too, old sins, bedraggled virtues, tarnished
Dreams, remembered unrealities, the gross
Should-haves, would-haves, the unvarnished
Errors of the day, burn, burn the loss
Of intentions, recurring failures, turn
Them all to ash. Incinerate the dross. Burn. Burn.

Summer City

Never have we had it so hot.
The children turn on hydrants
and the gutters run with sweat and garbage
and blood from the stupid sullen
so-called law that is only brutes
who feel the heat, too, I suppose,
and suffer as we, being, like us, flesh.
In the dark rats run over comfortless beds
and vermin crawl across the kitchen tables
and both come out on the street
and talk hate, stirring us up
like the putrid breeze
and anger begins to stir in our sluggish veins
and so we hate. We hate and are hungry for blood.
Never have we had it so hot.
One night a man came, stinking with sweat
like the rest of us, but different,
appearing, it seemed, from nowhere,
not out of the woodwork like the others.
So, for nothing better to do, we followed him
up three flights of urine-stinking stairs
to a room hot with many lights
and bodies crowded too close together.
I found no place to sit
but by then I was curious
and what else was there to do?
I climbed over steaming bodies
and found a seat on a paint-peeling sill
of an open window. He'd been talking awhile,

the man. I came in the middle
like walking into a movie and trying to guess
what must have gone on in the beginning
and missing things because of not knowing
what went on before. Why did I stay to listen?
He was ugly and I couldn't figure his angle.
He talked about some other man he loved
and when I jeered somebody said: shut up.
So I just stayed there in the open window.
I was tired and groggy from heat, and so I fell,
first asleep, and then, as he was long talking,
right out the sooty window, three floors down
onto the street. Well, it killed me:
I'm not kidding. I was dead. Then this man
rushed down the stairs, they tell me,
and they were crowding around me and shouting
and someone said call an ambulance,
and someone else (wanting a fight) said call the cops
and this man pushed his way through the mob
and flung himself on me and held me in his arms
close and warm, and told them not to worry
(though nobody gave a damn, it was just
something to get noisy about).
Then I sat up as though I had been asleep
and all I felt was hungry
so I walked back up those three putrid flights
of stairs and someone found some bread and cheese
and I ate, and drank some wine
and someone talked about the other men, the one
I'd jeered about, and then another guy called Lazarus,
and I didn't understand. I only knew

there was a difference in the room and if we went
back on the streets on stifling nights and listened
to the screams of *hate* and *kill*
there'd be no answering fury in my blood.
There was another way somewhere for me to find,
and this squat, ugly man,
talking amidst the filth, was showing me
although I didn't understand.
We talked a long while, even till break of day,
and then he went. And I was made alive
and not a little comforted.

Word

I, who live by words, am wordless when
I try my words in prayer. All language turns
To silence. Prayer will take my words and then
Reveal their emptiness. The stilled voice learns
To hold its peace, to listen with the heart
To silence that is joy, is adoration.
The self is shattered, all words torn apart
In this strange patterned time of contemplation
That, in time, breaks time, breaks words, breaks me,
And then, in silence, leaves me healed and mended.
I leave, returned to language, for I see
Through words, even when all words are ended.
   I, who live by words, am wordless when
   I turn me to the Word to pray. Amen.

From St. Luke's Hospital (2)

To my Guardian Angel

Beauty and form's singular absence
Has embarrassed me before the Power
Who made all loveliness. In the hour

When the Fall's result, dark ugliness,
Shakes my body, you, Angel, come,
Solid and familiar as a nanny in the room.

Thank you, Angel, for your presence
During all the vile indignities
That accompany body's dis-ease.

You hold the beauty of the images
Which make all creation sacrament,
Even this. Now there is no embarrassment.

Sustained by your stern confidence
In the holiness of all created things
I rest within the comfort of your wings.

The Monkey

Silence is dangerous.
We never permit it.
Our vocabulary may not be large
But there is no question that we put it
to constant use.
That's what things are for:
to be used. And used.
And used.
Who knows?
If we didn't talk and chatter from morning
till night (it doesn't matter
whether or not anybody listens; that's
not the point),
Words might start using us.
We never allow silence.
If sometimes it catches us unaware,
I am the first to screech across it
And shatter it to echoing fragments.
You never can tell:
if I listened to the silence
I might discover
that I am real.

Act III, Scene ii

Someone has altered the script.
My lines have been changed.
The other actors are shifting rôles.
They don't come on when they're expected to,
and they don't say the lines I've written
and I'm being upstaged.
I thought I was writing this play
with a rather nice rôle for myself,
small, but juicy
and some excellent lines.
But nobody gives me my cues
and the scenery has been replaced
and I don't recognize the new sets.
This isn't the script I was writing.
I don't understand this play at all.

To grow up
is to find
the small part you are playing
in this extraordinary drama
written by
somebody else.

Tree at Christmas

The children say the tree must reach the ceiling,
And so it does, angel on topmost branch,
Candy canes and golden globes and silver chains,
Trumpets that toot, and birds with feathered tails.
Each year we say, each year we fully mean:
"This is the loveliest tree of all." This tree
Bedecked with love and tinsel reaches heaven.
A pagan throwback may have brought it here
Into our room, and yet these decked-out boughs
Can represent those other trees, the one
Through which we fell in pride, when Eve forgot
That freedom is man's freedom to obey
And to adore, not to replace the light
With disobedient darkness and self-will.
On Twelfth Night when we strip the tree
And see its branches bare and winter cold
Outside the comfortable room, the tree
Is then the tree on which all darkness hanged,
Completing the betrayal that began
With that first stolen fruit. And then, O God,
This is the tree that Simon bore uphill,
This is the tree that held all love and life.
Forgive us, Lord, forgive us for that tree.
But now, still decked, bedecked, in joy arrayed
For these great days of Christmas thanks and song,
This is the tree that lights our faltering way,
For when man's first and proud rebellious act
Had reached its nadir on that hill of skulls
These shining, glimmering boughs remind us that

The knowledge that we stole was freely given
And we were sent the spirit's radiant strength
That we might know all things. We grasp for truth
And lose it till it comes to us by love.
The glory of Lebanon shines on this Christmas tree,
The tree of life that opens wide the gates.
The children say the tree must reach the ceiling,
And so it does: for me the tree has grown so high
It pierces through the vast and star-filled sky.

"The winter is cold, is cold"

The winter is cold, is cold.
All's spent in keeping warm.
Has joy been frozen, too?
I blow upon my hands
Stiff from the biting wind.
My heart beats slow, beats slow.
What has become of joy?

If joy's gone from my heart
Then it is closed to You
Who made it, gave it life.
If I protect myself
I'm hiding, Lord, from you.
How we defend ourselves
In ancient suits of mail!

Protected from the sword,
Shrinking from the wound,
We look for happiness,
Small, safety-seeking, dulled,
Selfish, exclusive, in-turned.
Elusive, evasive, peace comes
Only when it's not sought.

Help me forget the cold
That grips the grasping world.
Let me stretch out my hands

To purifying fire,
Clutching fingers uncurled.
Look! Here is the melting joy.
My heart beats once again.

Epithalamion:

Here at the time of a newer love's beginning
I see your body suddenly anew;
Each known and tempered touch, each sense and scent,
The strong and vulnerable and infinitely dear
Feel of the flesh that clothes your living bones
Wakens my body in the old and true response
Seen once again as miracle. To see you thus
As I have always seen you, but sometimes unaware,
Is unexpected grace. There is no part
Or portion that I do not love, but now
It is the human part, the fallen flesh
That wrenches me with startling pain and joy.
These bodies that will move to death, to dust,
Made, in an act of extraordinary grace
An explosion of light, a gift of life.
Now each expression that we make of love
Makes life anew, our lives a single life,
The two made one. In tenderness and play
We light the dark, and in this joyous game
We keep alight our candle's living flame.

Burn, Charity

Cold as charity, the saying goes:
I read it just now and it struck with the chill
Of the wind blowing in from the frozen river.
Cold as charity: the reluctant giver
Of love, the miser of self, cannot fill
Even himself with warmth. How the wind blows!

If I stand here in the cold I shall die
In this street of corpses and the grey near-dead.
Stone hands give out reluctant charity
And no one notices the wild disparity
Of the brilliant sun high overhead
Almost stilled by the clouds' chill cry.

My clothes keep out the heat of the sun!
I strip, I run from street to street
Chasing the distant sound of laughter,
Running, leaping, dancing after
The singing joy, my unshod feet
Glorying in the sun-warmed stone.

Naked, vulnerable, growing warm,
I meet another runner, arms spread wide
In loving and hilarious greeting.
The sun comes closer to light this meeting,
And shares our joyfulness as we stride
Laughing, exulting through wind and storm.

Nothing is everything to give,
A smile, a listening ear, a kiss,
Body and blood. Quick! Come and dine
On a crust of bread and the dregs of wine;
Never a feast was finer than this!
Come, eat and drink, unfreeze and live.

Body renewed and heart unfurled,
Love's banner blazes throughout the town
To twilight fear by law condemned,
To dayspring's joy by love redeemed.
Cold selfishness and dark be gone!
Burn, charity, and light the world!

The Dragon

Please, ma'am, my references are ample.
A small group of our family has always done domestic
    service.
Look at this recommendation; just a modest sample.
I know: my distant cousins make you nervous.

But think! I can replace all those machines in your
    residence.
You call that a stove! Well, just watch *me* boil water.
May I borrow that apron, please, and the kettle? Have no
    hesitance.
Watch. I spout a little flame. Fear not, I'll never eat your
    daughter.

I haven't fancied female flesh for years.
A touch more fire. See there? The kettle's boiling.
No, I'm a vegetarian now, eat modestly, make children
    laugh, dry tears,
Need little sleep, am not afraid of toiling,

Will save you fuel on your central heating.
I'm handy at making beds and sterilizing dishes.
These dusty rugs my tail is excellent at beating.
My disposition's sweet, and I grant wishes.

On winter nights when your feet are icy cold
I make a delightfully cozy foot warmer,
Can adjust my thermostat for young or old.
If burglars come I am a superb alarmer.

I guarantee I'll give you satisfaction.
Madam, I'm hurt! Unaccustomed to such dealings!
I cannot understand your rude reaction.
Remember that a dragon, too, has feelings.

From St. Luke's Hospital (3)

If I can learn a little how to die,
To die while body, mind, and spirit still
Move in their triune dance of unity,
To die while living, dying I'll fulfill
The purpose of the finite in infinity.
If God will help me learn to die today,
Today in time I'll touch eternity,
And dying, thus will live within God's Way.
If I can free myself from self's iron bands,
Freed from myself not by myself, but through
Christ's presence in this simple room, in hands
Outstretched in holy friendship, then, born new
In death, truth will outlive the deathly lie,
And in love's light I will be taught to die.

Within This Strange and Quickened Dust

O God, within this strange and quickened dust
The beating heart controls the coursing blood
In discipline that holds in check the flood
But cannot stem corrosion and dark rust.
In flesh's solitude I count it blest
That only you, my Lord, can see my heart
With passion's darkness tearing it apart
With storms of self, and tempests of unrest.
But your love breaks through blackness, bursts with light;
We separate ourselves, but you rebind
In Dayspring all our fragments; body, mind,
And spirit join, unite against the night.
Healed by your love, corruption and decay
Are turned, and whole, we greet the light of day.

Song of Simeon

When I was younger
Christmas was clearer
Magic was stronger
Santa Claus nearer.
He came from the North Pole
With reindeer wild
Bearing his soul
For the young Christ-child,
And toys and baubles
His elves had wrought
To take away troubles
And set them at naught.
An angel flew by him
To sit on the tree
And cherubs did cry him
And glory was three.
But now I am older
And Santa's a vagrant
On a street colder,
More crowded, less fragrant
Of pine cones and holly
And loving and laughter.
There's naught left but folly
And the bitter taste after.
I stand on a corner
Ringing a bell,
A red-suited mourner
Staving off hell
With a cupful of pennies

To throw on the table
Oh where and oh when is
The child in the stable
Coming to bring us
The tears that are mirth?
Come, angels, sing us
The death that is birth.

The Parrot

It was better in the jungle.
There I could imitate
the sound of dawn.
I could speak with the voice
of many tongues
and even if I didn't understand
I was still, in a sense,
an interpreter.
I could call with the song
of setting stars.
I could whisper with the leaves
before rain.

It is not the cage
that prisons me.
I, who live by mimicry,
have become made
in the image of man.

From St. Luke's Hospital (4)

Good Samaritan

She comes on at night,
older than middle-aged, from the islands,
to answer the patients' bells
to see if it's worth disturbing an overworked nurse.
At first she was suspicious, cross,
expecting complaints and impositions,
soon tender and gentle,
concerned about requests for help with pain,
coming in (without being asked)
with a blanket if it turned cold,
hoping, as she said goodbye
at the night's end, for a good day.
This morning she rushed in, frantic,
please, please could she look for the money
she had lost somehow, tending patients,
forty dollars that was not even hers.
She had kept it, in time-honored tradition,
in her bosom, and it must have fallen out
when she was thinking of someone else's needs.
She scrabbled in the wastebasket,
in the bedclothes, panted from room to room,
returned to mine with a friend. We said,
"Close the door, take off your clothes, and see
if it isn't still on you somewhere."
She did, revealing an overworked body,
wrinkled, scarred; found nothing; had to leave.
She's off now, for a week. I'll never know

if she found it or not; will remember
her kindness and her panic. O God,
here, as so often, I cannot help.
Let me not forget she is your child
and your concern makes mine as nothing.
All I can do, and this I do, is love, is pray.

Lines After M. B.'s Funeral

There's a hole in the world.
I'm afraid I may fall through.
Someone has died
Was
Has gone
Is where?
Will be
Is
How?
This is neither the first
Nor the only time that space has opened.
We are riddled with death
Like a sieve.
The dark holes are as multitudinous
As the stars in the galaxies,
As open to the cold blasts of wind.
If we fell through
What would we find?
Show me
Let me look through this new empty space
To where
The wind comes from
And the light begins.

The Sea Bishop

The waves, the tides, the ocean: all in tune.
Raised from the sea my pale and ancient hand
Sprays benedictions from my silver wand.
How tender now the blessing of the moon.
Raised from the sea my pale and ancient hand
Absolves all creatures of the sea and dune
(How tender now the blessing of the moon)
The birds, the shellfish, water things, and land,

Absolves all creatures of the sea and dune,
The soaring dolphin by pure moonbeams fanned,
The birds, the shellfish, water things, and land.
Across the stars the wind sweeps out its tune.
On the white whale small flecks of silver stand
Caught by the light from soaring fountain spewn.
Across the stars the wind sweeps out its tune
For all my creatures, sky, and sea, and land.

Confession Shortly Before the Forty-eighth Birthday

Here I am, beyond the middle middle,
According to chronology,
No closer to solving cosmic or private riddle,
No further from apology
For clumsy self's continuing ineptitude,
Still shaken by the heart's wild battering.
Intemperate passions constantly intrude;
I cannot keep small hurts from mattering,
Am shattered when met with mild irritation,
Need reassurance, feel inadequate and foolish,
Seek love's return, bump into abrogation,
Am stubborn beyond the point of being merely mulish.
So am I saved only by the strange stern power of silence,
The disciplined joy of work and rule
Inner and outer imposed, steel cold. The violence
Of the freezing wind sustains the heart. So this poor fool
Is fed, is nourished, forgets then to be concerned with
    rust;
Repentance, too, is turning, if towards dust,
And gratitude sings forth in adoration
Of the one who touched and healed the halt and lame
With the aweful, blissful power of his spoken Name.

FROM
THE IRRATIONAL
SEASON

(1977)

"Let us view with joy and mirth"

Let us view with joy and mirth
All the clocks upon the earth
    Holding time with busy tocking
    Ticking booming clanging clocking
       Anxiously unraveling
       Time's traveling
Through the stars and winds and tides.
Who can tell where time abides?

Foolish clocks, all time was broken
When that first great Word was spoken.
    Cease we now this silly fleeing
    From earth's time, for time's a being
       And adoring
       Bows before him
Who upon the throne is seated.
Time, defeated, wins, is greeted.

Clocks know not time's loving wonder
Day above as night swings under,
    Turning always to the son,
    Time's begun, is done, does run
       Singing warning
       Of the morning
Time, mass, space, a mystery
Of eternal trinity.

Time needs make no poor apology
For bursting forth from man's chronology

Laughs in glee as human hours
Dance before the heavenly powers.
 Time's undone
 Because the Son
Swiftly calls the coming light
That will end the far-spent night.

"As I grow older"

As I grow older
I get surer
Man's heart is colder,
His life no purer.
As I grow steadily
More austere
I come less readily
To Christmas each year.
I can't keep taking
Without a thought
Forced merrymaking
And presents bought
In crowds and jostling.
Alas, there's naught
In empty wassailing
Where oblivion's sought.
Oh, I'd be waiting
With quiet fasting
Anticipating
A joy more lasting.
And so l rhyme
With no apology
During this time
Of eschatology:
Judgment and warning
Come like thunder.
But now is the hour
When I remember

An infant's power
On a cold December.
Midnight is dawning
And the birth of wonder.

. . . And the Old Man Became as a Little Child . . .

He could not sleep.
The tomb was dark, and the stone heavy that sealed it.
He could not sleep for all the innocent blood he had seen
    shed.
He was an old man. Too old for tears.
Not yet young enough for sleep. He waited and watched.

Thrice he had spoken to him whose body had been sealed
within the tomb, thrice had the old man spoken,
he who was a disciple, but not one of the twelve,
older, gentler in all ways,
and tired, worn with time and experience and the
    shedding of blood.
He came from Capernaum
and after that his son
who touched the edge of death
was drawn back from the pit
and made whole,
the old man returned to Jesus and said,
"O thou, who hast today been the consolation of my
    household,
wast also its desolation.
Because of you my first-born died
in that great shedding of innocent blood.
Nevertheless, I believe
though I know not what
or how or why
for it has not been revealed to me.

I only know that one manchild was slain
and one made to live."

And a second time he spoke
when the Lord kept the children beside him
and suffered them not to be taken away:
"These are the ones that are left us,
but where, Lord, is the Kingdom of Heaven?
Where, Lord, are the others?
What of them? What of them?"
And he wept.

And a third time he spoke
when the Lord turned to Jerusalem
and laughter turned to steel
and he moved gravely
towards the hour that was prepared
and the bitterness of the cup:
then the old man said,
"All your years you have lived
under the burden of their blood.
Their life was the price of yours.
Have you borne the knowledge and the cost?
During those times
when you have gone silent in the midst of laughter
have you remembered all the innocence
slaughtered that you might be with us now?
When you have gone up into the mountain apart to pray,
have you remembered that their lives were cut down
for your life, and so ours?
Rachel's screams still shatter the silence

and I cannot sleep at night for remembering.
Do you ever forget your children that sleep?
When will you bring them out of the sides of the earth
and show mercy unto them?
Who will embrace them until you come?
I cannot sleep.
But because I have already tasted of the cup
I cannot turn from you now.
I, who live, praise you.
Can those who have gone before you into the pit
celebrate you or hope for your truth?
Tell me, tell me, for I am an old man
and lost in the dark cloud of my ignorance.
Nevertheless, blessed is he
whom thou hast chosen and taken, O Lord."

He did not speak again.

But he was there when the rocks were rent
the veil of the temple torn in twain
the sun blackened by clouds
the earth quaked with darkness

the sky was white and utterly empty.
The city gaped with loss.
Then, out of the silence,
the Lord went
bearing the marks of nails and spear
moving swiftly through the darkness
into the yawning night of the pit.
There he sought first

not as one might have supposed
for Moses or Elias
but for the children
who had been waiting for him.
So, seeking, he was met
by the three Holy Children
the Young Men
burning bright
transforming the fire into dew as they cried:
"Blessed art thou, O Lord God, forevermore."

And all the children came running
and offering to him their blood
and singing: "With sevenfold heat
did the Chaldean tyrant in his rage
cause the furnace to be heated
for the Godly Ones
who wiped our blood like tears
when we were thrust here
lost and unknowing.
The Holy Three
waited here to receive us
and to teach us to sing your coming
forasmuch as thou art pitiful
and lovest mankind."
So they held his hand
and gave him their kisses and their blood
and, laughing, led him by the dragon
who could not bear their innocence
and thrashed with his tail
so that the pit trembled with his rage.

But even his roaring could not drown their song:
"For unto Thee are due all glory, honor, and worship,
with the Father and the Holy Spirit, now, and ever,
and unto ages of ages, Amen."

And the holy children were round about him,
the Holy Innocents and the Holy Three.
They walked through the darkness of the fiery furnace
and the dragon could see their brightness,
yea, he saw four walkers loose
walking in the midst of the fire and having no hurt
and the form of the fourth was like the Son of God.

And he saw the Son of God move through hell
and he heard the Holy Children sing:
"Meet is it that we should magnify thee,
the life-giver
who has stretched out thy hands upon the cross
and hast shattered the dominion of the enemy.
Blessed art thou, O Lord God, forevermore.

O Jesus, God and Saviour,
who didst take upon thee Adam's sin
and didst taste of death
(the cup was bitter),
thou hast come again to Adam
O compassionate One
for thou only art good
and lovest mankind,
Blessed art thou, O Lord God, forevermore."

So hell was shriven
while the holy children, singing,
transformed the flames to dew,
and the gates of Heaven opened.

Then, by the empty tomb,
the old man slept.

On Valentine's Day, for a Saint Most Misunderstood

He was a strange old man
given to solitude on the forest,
eating acorns and locusts.
When he saw a young virgin
he ceased baying at the moon,
lay down, and put his head in her lap.

He helped the sun rise every morning
and pulled the ocean high on the shore
at each full moon. He knew that love
is like a sword. He felt its pain.
His blood fell on the snow and turned to roses
and so he was, of all saints, most misunderstood.

His eyes are flame, and their look sears.
We pretend he's someone else to avoid burning.
I would go into the forest, silent and alone.
If I find him, will he dry my tears?

"Boarding school: someone cried jubilantly"

Boarding school: someone cried jubilantly,
"There's a letter for you! Didn't you see it?"

The letter was from my mother. My father
was in the hospital with pneumonia.
This was the autumn before the miracle drugs were
    discovered.
In any case, his lungs were already half eaten away from
    mustard gas.

I did not tell anyone. I tried to pray. Perhaps I knew how
    better then than now.
I only whispered God's name; then, Father; then, God.

In the evenings we did our lessons in a basement room
    with many desks,
and windows looking out on the Charleston street.
Little black boys with wildly painted faces and bobbing
    jack-o'lanterns
peered in on us and shrieked, and their laughter
is all I remember of Hallowe'en.

I sent Father a poem, knowing it would not reach him in
    time.

The next afternoon the headmistress sent for me; my
    father was very ill.
I was to take the train right after the evening meal.

It was the night when the Head Girl was to say grace.
    How odd
that I should remember it, and that all that seemed
    important
was that my voice be steady.

One of the teachers took me to the train.
I tried to read *Jane Eyre*.

When my parents had put me on the train for school
my last words as I climbed up the high step onto the train
    were to my father:
"Be good." I remember: the last words, and my father
    standing
on the station platform in a rain-darkened trench coat,
    and the rain
beating on the dirty glass of the station roof
so that we saw each other only darkly.

I tried to read *Jane Eyre* and to pray to the rhythm of the
    wheels:
Please, God, do whatever is best for Father. Please, God,
    do whatever

is best
please
God

My two Godmothers met me. I asked, "How is Father?"
It took the whole drive home before they told me.
I was taken to see my father in the manner of the times.

I did not know him.
I closed my eyes and stood there
seeing him better, then.

My mother and I talked quite calmly
about things like toothpaste.
I remember that. I did not cry.
It was thought that I did not care.

I was a human being and a young one.
We cannot always cry at the right time
and who is to say which time is right?

I did not cry till three years later
when I first fell, most inappropriately,
in love.
But I began, after the tears,
to know my father.

When we are grown up enough
compassed about with so great a cloud of witnesses
that we are not afraid of tears
then at last
we can say
Father
I love you
Father.

"Who shoved me out into the night?"

Who shoved me out into the night?
What wind blew out the quavering light?
Is it my breath, undone with fright?
    This is the Kingdom of the Beast.
    For which will I provide the feast?

Who once was daft, with fear am dafter.
Who went before? Who will come after?
Who in this darkness sends me laughter?
    I cannot pray, but I am prayed,
    The prey prepared, bedecked, arrayed.

The dark is sound against my ear,
Is loud with clatter of my fear.
I hear soft footsteps padding near.
    I, who have fed, will be the eaten,
    Whose dinner will I sour or sweeten?

This is not hell, nor say I damn.
I know not who nor why I am
But I am walking with a lamb
    And all the tears that ever were
    Are gently dried on his soft fur,

And tears that never could be shed
Are held within that tender head.
Tears quicken now that once were dead.
    O little lamb, how you do weep
    For all the strayed and stricken sheep.

Your living fur against my hand
You guide me in this unseen land,
And still I do not understand.
   The darkness deepens more and more
   Till it is shattered by a roar.

Lamb, stop! Don't leave me here alone
For this wild beast to call his own,
To kill, to shatter, flesh and bone.
   Against the dark I whine and cower.
   I fear the lion. I dread his hour.

Here is the slap of unsheathed paws.
I feel the tearing of his claws,
Am shaken in his mighty jaws.
   This dark is like a falcon's hood
   Where is my flesh and where my blood?

The lamb has turned to lion, wild,
With nothing tender, gentle, mild,
Yet once again I am a child,
   A babe newborn, a fresh creation,
   Flooded with joy, swept by elation.

Those powerful jaws have snapped the tether,
Have freed me to the wind and weather.
O Lion, let us run together,
   Free, willing now to be untame,
   Lion, you are light: joy is in flame.

O Hilaritas

According to Newton
the intrinsic property of matter on which weight depends is
mass.
But mass and weight vary according to gravity
(It is not a laughing matter).
On earth a mass of 6 kilograms has a weight of
      6 kilograms.
On the moon a mass of 6 kilograms has a weight of
      1 kilogram.
An object's inertia (the force required to accelerate it)
depends entirely on its mass.
And so with me.
I depend entirely on a crumb of bread
a sip of wine;
it is the mass that matters
that makes matter.
In free fall, like the earth around the sun,
I am weightless
and so move only if I have mass.
Thanks be to the creator
who has given himself
that we may be.

"How very odd it seems, dear Lord"

How very odd it seems, dear Lord,
That when I go to seek your Word
In varied towns at home, abroad,
I'm in the company of the absurd.

The others who come, as I do,
Starving for need of sacrament,
Who sit beside me in the pew,
Are both in mind and body bent.

I kneel beside the old, unfit,
The young, the lonely stumbling few,
And I myself, with little wit,
Hunger and thirst, my God, for you.

I share communion with the halt,
The lame, the blind, oppressed, depressed.
We have, it seems, a common fault
In coming to you to be blessed.

And my fit friends, intelligent,
Heap on my shoulders a strange guilt.
Are only fools and sinners meant
To come unto you to be filled?

Among the witless and absurd
I flee to find you and to share
With eyes and ears and lips your Word.
I pray, my God. God, hear my prayer.

From city streets and lanes we come.
I slip unto you like a thief
To be with you, at peace, at home,
Lord, I believe. Oh, help my unbelief.

Great and Holy Saturday

Death and damnation began with my body still my own,
began when I was ousted from my place,
and many creatures still were left unnamed.
Gone are some, now, extinct, and nameless,
as though they had never been.
In hell I feel their anxious breath, see their accusing eyes.
My guilt is heavier than was the weight of flesh.
I bear the waste of time spent in recriminations
("You should not have. . . ." "But you told me. . . ." "Nay,
        it was you who. . . .").
And yet I knew my wife, and this was good.
But all good turned to guilt. Our first-born
killed his brother. Only Seth gave us no grief.
I grew old, and was afraid; afraid to die, even knowing
that death had come, and been endured, when we
were forced to leave our home, the one and only home a
        human man
has ever known. The rest is exile.
Death, when it came, was no more than a dim
continuation of the exile. I was hardly less a shadow
than I had been on earth, and centuries
passed no more slowly than a single day.
I was not prepared to be enfleshed again,
reconciled, if not contented, with my shadow self.
I had seen the birth of children with all its blood and pain
and had no wish ever to be born again.

The sound, when it came, was louder than thunder,
louder than the falling of a mountain,
louder than the tidal wave crashing down the city walls,
stone splitting, falling, smashing.
The light was brutal against my shaded eyes,
blinding me with brilliance. I was thousands
of years unaccustomed to the glory.
Then came the wrench of bone where bone had long been
        dust.
The shocking rise of dry bones, the burning fleshing,
the surge of blood through artery and vein
was pain as I had never known that pain could be.
My anguished scream was silenced as my hand was held
in a grip of such authority I could not even try to pull
        away.
The crossed gates were trampled by his powerful feet
and I was wrenched through the chasm
as through the eye of the hurricane.
And then—O God—he crushed me
in his fierce embrace. Flesh entered flesh;
bone, bone. Thus did I die, at last.
Thus was I born.
Two Adams became one.
And in the glory Adam was.
Nay, Adam is.

"Seeking perspective in a hate-torn world"

Seeking perspective in a hate-torn world,
Leaving, for respite brief, the choking city,
I turn to trees, new leaves not quite unfurled,
A windswept blue-pure sky for pity.
Across a pasture, over a stone wall,
Past berry brambles and an unused field,
Listening for leaf sound and the brook's clear call,
Turning down path by bush and tree concealed,
Forgetting human sin and nature's fall
I seek perfection in the cool green still.
Small trees with new spring growth are tall.
Here is no sign of human hate or ill.
    Unexpecting any pain or shock
    I turn to climb upon my thinking rock.

The rock stands high above the snow-full brook.
Behind the rock an old tree breaks the sky,
And on the tree where bird and beast may look
An icon and a cross are hanging high.
So strong are they, placed lovingly together,
I need have little fear for their protection
Through wind and snow and bitter wintry weather.
They speak to me of joy and Resurrection
And here my self-will stills, my heart beats slow.
God's presence in his world is bright and strong.
Upon the rock I climb, and then—No! No!
The sky is dark and here is hate and wrong.
    O God! Make it not be! Oh, make it not!
    The icon: target for a rifle's shot.

A wave of dark blasts cold across my face.
My stomach heaves with nausea at the dirt
Of hate in this pure green and loving place.
The trees pull back and cower in their hurt.
Rooted, they could not stop the vicious gun
Fired straight at God's birth-giver and her child.
There's only death in this. It's no one's fun
To blaspheme love. A shot has made a wild
Distortion of the young and ancient face.
I give the broken fragments to the brook
And let the water lap them with its grace.
And then I sit upon the rock and look
    At the great gouge in the tree's wood.
    Evil obscures all peace and love and good.

As I sit looking at the shot-at tree
The rough wound opens and grows strange and deep
Within the wood, till suddenly I see
A galaxy aswirl with flame. I do not sleep
And yet I see a trillion stars speed light
In ever-singing dance within the hole
Surrounded by the tree. Each leaf's alight
With flame. And then a burning living coal
Drops hissing in the brook, and all the suns
Burst outward in their joy, and the shot child,
Like the great and flaming tree, runs
With fire and water, and alive and wild
    Gentle and strong, becomes the wounded tree.
    Lord God! The icon's here, alive and free.

All That Matters

Nothing.
Out of nothing
out of the void
(what?
where?)
God created.

Out of
Nothing
which is
what?
But it is
not a what
or a where
or an opposite
of something
or anything.
Nothing is
nothing
we can know.
Does it matter
that matter's mind
must not mind
not knowing
nothing
doubly negatively
or in any way
positively
not.

O Mind
that alone knows
nothing
O Word
that speaks
to matter
that
speaks matter
from the unspoken:
that you mind
is all that matters.

"Go away. You can't come in. I'm shutting the door."

Go away. You can't come in. I'm shutting the door.
I'm afraid of you. I'm not sure who you are anymore.
I'm closing the door. I'm staying safe and alone.
Batter against it all you like. This house is built on stone.
You can't come in. I've shuttered the windows tight.
You never say who you are. If it's You, then it's all right,
But you might be the other, the beautiful prince of this
    world
Who makes my heart leap with his cohorts and banners
    unfurled.
I could be unfaithful with him without any trouble
If I opened the door. He could easily pass for your double.
I've buried my talents. If I put them to use
I could hurt or be hurt, be abused or abuse.
I wish you'd stop blowing. My whole house is shaken.
I'll hide under the covers. Be gone when I waken.

What's that light at the windows, that blast at the door?
The shutters are burning, there's fire on the floor.
Go away. I don't know you. My clothes are aflame,
My tongue is on fire, you are crying my name;
I hear your wild voice through the holocaust's din.
My house is burned up.
                    What?
                    Oh, welcome! Come in!

"Now we may love the child"

Now we may love the child.
Now he is ours,
this tiny thing,
utterly vulnerable and dependent
on the circle of our love.
Now we may hold him,
feeling with gentle hands
the perfection of his tender skin
from the soft crown of his head
to the sweet soles of his merrily kicking feet.
His fingers softly curl
around one finger of the grownup hand.
Now we may hold.
Now may I feel his hungry sucking at my breast
as I give him my own life.
Now may my husband toss him in the air
and catch him in his sure and steady hands
laughing with laughter as quick and pure
as the baby's own.
Now may I rock him softly to his sleep,
rock and sing,
sing and hold.
This moment of time is here,
has happened, is:
rejoice!
Child,
give me the courage
for the time
when I must open my arms
and let you go.

"When I pushed through the crowd"

When I pushed through the crowd,
jostled, bumped, elbowed by the curious
who wanted to see what everyone else
was so excited about,
all I could think of was my pain
and that perhaps if I could touch him,
this man who worked miracles,
cured diseases,
even those as foul as mine,
I might find relief.
I was tired from hurting,
exhausted, revolted by my body,
unfit for any man, and yet not let loose
from desire and need. I wanted to rest,
to sleep without pain or filthiness or torment.
I don't really know why
I thought he could help me
when all the doctors
with all their knowledge
had left me still drained
and bereft of all that makes
a woman's life worth living.
Well: I'd seen him with some children
and his laughter was quick and merry
and reminded me of when I was young and well,
though he looked tired; and he was as old as I am.
Then there was that leper,
but lepers have been cured before—

No, it wasn't the leper,
or the man cured of palsy,
or any of the other stories of miracles,
or at any rate that was the least of it;
I had been promised miracles too often.
I saw him ahead of me in the crowd
and there was something in his glance
and in the way his hand rested briefly
on the matted head of a small boy
who was getting in everybody's way,
and I knew that if only I could get to him,
not to bother him, you understand,
not to interrupt, or to ask him for anything,
not even his attention,
just to get to him and touch him . . .

I didn't think he'd mind, and he needn't even know.
I pushed through the crowd
and it seemed that they were deliberately
trying to keep me from him.
I stumbled and fell and someone stepped
on my hand and I cried out
and nobody heard. I crawled to my feet
and pushed on and at last I was close,
so close I could reach out
and touch with my fingers
the hem of his garment.

Have you ever been near
when lightning struck?
I was, once, when I was very small

and a summer storm came without warning
and lightning split the tree
under which I had been playing
and I was flung right across the courtyard.
That's how it was.
Only this time I was not the child
but the tree
and the lightning filled me.
He asked, "Who touched me?"
and people dragged me away, roughly,
and the men around him were angry at me.

"Who touched me?" he asked.
I said, "I did, Lord,"
So that he might have the lightning back
which I had taken from him when I touched
his garment's hem.
He looked at me and I knew then
that only he and I knew about the lightning.
He was tired and emptied
but he was not angry.
He looked at me
and the lightning returned to him again,
though not from me, and he smiled at me
and I knew that I was healed.
Then the crowd came between us
and he moved on, taking the lightning with him,
perhaps to strike again.

"The children at the party"

The children at the party
sit in a circle playing games,
rhythm games, singing games, clapping games,
and finally the whispering game:
the little girl in the white organdy dress and blue sash
whispers a sentence to the little boy in grey flannel shorts
and he in turn whispers it to the little girl on his right
and so it goes all the way around the circle
round and round
as the earth whirls round the sun
and the sun swings in the great circle of the galaxy
    he is risen
    we thought he was the one who
    we thought it was he
    he is risen
    he is exactly like us but sinless
    not like us then
    sinful
    he is risen
    three in one
    and one in three
    and the great hawk cracks the sky
    he in us
    we in him
    bread and wine
    ashes to ashes
    and
    dust to dust

he is risen
is he

And the sentence returns to the little girl
and she says the nonsense words aloud
and everybody laughs and no one understands.

"It is an old church"

It is an old church,
two hundred years old,
and that is old for this gawky country
though perhaps young by other standards.
The congregation today (as in most churches)
is sparse.
In the old New England tradition
we amble into our seats
and only a few outsiders
indulge in the impropriety and popery
of bowing their heads in prayer
(nobody would dare kneel).
So of course nobody remembers that this is
the time of the rushing wind and the tongues of fire.
Today is the Sunday when the Young People's Group,
the Pilgrim Fellowship, is going to lead the worship.
They are dressed in jeans, shirts—
the girls as well as the boys—
and someone puts on a record
and in the chancel they dance to the music
separately
(nobody touches anybody else)
and not very well. But it is Their Own Thing,
their response:
two women get up and leave the church.
Then one of the girls goes to the lectern (she brought me a
        kitten once)
and tells us that they are not there to shock us
but to tell us what is on their minds.

Another girl talks about the importance of individualism;
what she really means is that she cares
about the fall of the sparrow
and the gloriously unutterable value of persons.
But somebody else walks out.
Then a boy (his mother and I were pregnant
together with our sons; I have seen him
learn to walk and talk)
gets up and says he does not believe in God
or life after death
or anything he's been taught in Sunday School.
If there is a God, he says,
we have to find him where we live,
and he finds church when he walks alone
in the woods.
There is a movement in the back of the church
as someone else leaves.
Then our nearest neighbors' boy,
our son's close friend,
talking too fast in his urgency,
cries out against war
and napalm
and job recruiters for Dow Chemical
and killing killing killing
and more people walk out.
Then the young people (still trying) come to
pass the Peace
and they put on another record and sing to it
and they CARE
And someone else leaves

oh stop
oh stop
STOP

This is Pentecost
the wind is blowing
the flames are bright
the Spirit burns

O stop
listen
all you Parthians, Medes, Elamites,
dwellers in Mesopotamia, Judea, Cappadocia,
in Pontus, and Asia, Phrygia and Pamphylia, in Egypt
and in the parts of Libya around Cyrene,
O stop
strangers of Rome, Jews and proselytes, Cretes and
Arabians, dwellers in New England, New York,
Indiana, India, California, Chile,
China, Russia, Africa.

Stop and listen
to these children who speak in your own tongue
the wonderful works of God.

"Rejoice!"

Rejoice!
You have just given me the universe,
put it in my hands, held it to my lips,
oh, here on my knees have I been fed
the entire sum of all created matter,
the everything
that came from nothing.
Rejoice!
Who can doubt its power?
Did not this crumb of bread
this sip of wine
burst into life
that thundered across nothing
and became the cause of all our
celebrations?
Oh, the explosion of nothing into something,
into flaming, raging suns and shouting comets
and drops of dew and spiders' webs
into mountains bursting forth with brilliant volcanoes
valleys falling and rising
laughing with joy
earth's cracking, primordial rains flooding
a snowdrop's star, a baby's cry
oh, rejoice!
rejoice and celebrate
eyes to see and ears to hear
fingers to touch
to touch
the body's living warmth

hand stretched to hand
across nothing
making something
celebrate
lips to smile
to kiss
to take the bread and wine
rejoice
flowers   grass   pavements
gutters   garbage cans
old people remembering
babies laughing
mothers singing
fathers celebrating
rejoice
around the table
hold hands
all round
like a ring circling a finger
placed there as a promise
holding the universe together
nothing into something
into joy and love
rejoice
and celebrate!

"Silence was the one thing we were not prepared for"

Silence was the one thing we were not prepared for,
we are never prepared for.
Silence is too much like death.
We do not understand it.
Whenever it comes we make up thunders and lightnings
and we call anxiously for the angels to sing for us.
It is all right for Elijah to kill all those false prophets,
though they were comfortingly noisy;
it is all right for him to bring that poor widow's boy
back to life with his own audible breath;
that is only a miracle. We understand miracles.
But he survived God's silence, and that is more
        extraordinary
than all the sounds of all of Israel's battles rolled into one.
Why is God silent? Why does he not sound for us?
He came silently to birth. Only the angels,
Taking pity on us, sang to make that silence bearable.
When he came to dwell among us men on earth
only his mother understood the silence,
and when he died she made no sound of weeping.
Why does silence make us shiver with the fear of death?
There was more sound to comfort our ears
when he was hammered to the cross
and cried out through the strangling bonds
and the temple veil was rent and graves burst wide,
than when he was born. I am not sure
that death is silent. But Easter is.
The angels did not sing for us, heralding the glory.

There was no sound to prepare us, no noise of miracle,
no trumpet announcing the death of death—
or was it what we call life? We did not understand
and we ran from the empty tomb and then
he came to us in silence. He did not explain
and at last I knew that only in silence is the word
even when the word itself is silent.

Thus in silence did that strange dark bird
Bring to Elijah in the desert the whole and holy Word.

Love Letter Addressed To:

Your immanent eminence
wholly transcendent
permanent, in firmament
holy, resplendent
other and aweful
incomprehensible
legal, unlawful
wild, indefensible
eminent immanence
mysterium tremendum
mysterium fascinans
incarnate, trinitarian
being impassible
infinite wisdom
one indivisible
king of the kingdom
logos, word-speaker
star-namer, narrator
man-maker, man-seeker
ex nihil creator
unbegun, unbeginning
complete but unending
wind-weaving, sun-spinning
ruthless, unbending:
Eternal compassion
helpless before you
I, Lord, in my fashion,
love and adore you.

"Sitting around your table"

Sitting around your table
as we did, able
to laugh, argue, share
bread and wine and companionship, care
about what someone else was saying, even
if we disagreed passionately: Heaven,
we're told, is not unlike this, the banquet celestial,
eternal convivium. So the praegustum terrestrium
partakes—for me, at least—of sacrament.
(Whereas the devil, ever intent
on competition, invented the cocktail party where
one becomes un-named, un-manned, de-personned.) Dare
we come together, then, vulnerable, open, free?
Yes! Around your table we
knew the Holy Spirit, come to bless
the food, the host, the hour, the willing guest.

"This is a strange place"

This is a strange place
and I would be lost were it not for all the others
who have been here before me.
It is the alien space
of your absence.
It has been called, by some,
the dark night of the soul.
But it is absence of dark as well as light,
an odd emptiness,
the chill of any land without your presence.
And yet, in this Lent of your absence,
I am more certain of your love and comfort
than when it is I who have withdrawn from you.

Mrs. Noah Speaking

I suppose under the circumstances
there's really no point in complaining
but really! Noah and I had just got accustomed
to living alone and having some peace and quiet
and fixing up the house the way we wanted it at last.
I brought up three boys, wiped their runny noses,
    changed their messy diapers,
  washed, sewed, cooked, saw to it that they had the
    proper advantages,
We got them safely married
  (though if I didn't know it before I know it now: their
    wives leave a great deal to be desired).
We liked having them come to visit us on the proper
    holidays,
  bringing the babies, taking enough food home to feed
    them for a week,
  and Noah and I could go to bed in peace.
And now look what has happened!

Sometimes I think it would have been simpler to have
    drowned with everybody else—
at least their troubles are over.
And here we are jammed in this Ark—
why didn't the Lord give Noah enough time to build a big
    enough ark
  if he wanted him to build one at all?
The animals take up almost all the room
and Noah and I are crowded together with Shem, Ham,
    and Japheth, their slovenly wives and noisy children,

and nowhere to go for a moment's peace.
Noah, of course, has hidden several elephant's skins of
    wine somewhere,
  and when the rain and noise and confusion get too bad
  he goes down to the dirty hold with the beasts and gets
    drunk,
  sleeps it off on the dirty straw,
  and then comes up to bed smelling of armadillo dung
    and platypus piss.

Not that I blame him.
It's my daughters-in-law who get me.
They insist on changing the beds every time I turn
    around.
They won't use a towel more than once, and they're always
    getting dressed up
  and throwing their dirty linen at me to wash.
The washing is easy enough—we've plenty of water—
But how do they expect me to get anything dry in all this
    rain?
I don't mind doing the cooking, but they're always
    coming out to the kitchen to fix little snacks with the
    excuse that it will help me: "You're so good to us,
    Mother Noah, we'll just do this for you," and they
    never put anything away where it belongs. They've
    lost one of my measuring cups and they never clean
    the stove and they've broken half of the best china
    that came down to us from Grandfather Seth.
When the babies squall in the night, who gets up with
    them?
Not my daughters-in-law.

"Oh, Mother Noah'll do it. She loves the babies so."
Ham's wife is always stirring up quarrels, playing people
off against each other. Shem's wife, who never does
anything for anybody, manages to make me feel lazy
and mean if I ask her to dry one dish. Japheth's wife
is eyeing Shem and Ham; she'll cause trouble; mark
my words.

Today that silly dove Noah is so fond of came back with
an olive twig on his beak. Maybe there's hope that
we'll get out of this Ark after all.

We've landed! At last! Now we can get back to normal and
have some peace and quiet and if I put something
where it belongs it will stay there and I can clean up
this mess and get some sleep at night and—

Noah! Noah! I miss the children.

"Suddenly they saw him the way he was"

Suddenly they saw him the way he was
the way he really was all the time,
although they had never seen it before,
the glory which blinds the everyday eye
and so becomes invisible. This is how
he was, radiant, brilliant, carrying joy
like a flaming sun in his hands.
This is the way he was—is—from the beginning,
and we cannot bear it. So he manned himself,
came manifest to us; and there on the mountain
they saw him, really saw him, saw his light.
We all know that if we really see him we die.
But isn't that what is required of us?
Then, perhaps, we will see each other, too.

The Air Bites Shrewdly

There is almost nothing a child cannot bear
As long as the image of its parent shines clear.
Age is acceptable, normal wear and tear,
But poison cannot fall into the ear.
The image distorts; safety is gone; is where?

Hamlet, after the death of his father,
Found, also, changes in his mother,
And it was this latter, rather,
It would seem to me, than the other
That caused the dark storm clouds to gather.

The person changed is blackly unacceptable
(Primeval fears of presence of a devil);
Soma, not psyche, may be corruptible.
How does the distorted one find grace in this black evil?
Help my mother to bear. God, make her able.

"Come, Lord Jesus, quickly come"

Come, Lord Jesus, quickly come
In your fearful innocence.
We fumble in the far-spent night
Far from lovers, friends, and home:
Come in your naked, newborn might.
Come, Lord Jesus, quickly come;
My heart withers in your absence.

Come, Lord Jesus, small, enfleshed
Like any human, helpless child.
Come once, come once again, come soon:
The stars in heaven fall, unmeshed;
The sun is dark, blood's on the moon.
Come, word who came to us enfleshed,
Come speak in joy untamed and wild.

Come, thou wholly other, come,
Spoken before words began,
Come and judge your uttered world
Where you made our flesh your home.
Come, with bolts of lightning hurled,
Come, thou wholly other, come,
Who came to man by being man.

Come, Lord Jesus, at the end,
Time's end, my end, forever's start.
Come in your flaming, burning power.

Time, like the temple veil, now rend;
Come, shatter every human hour.
Come, Lord Jesus, at the end.
Break, then mend the waiting heart.

FROM *THE WEATHER* OF *THE HEART*

(1978)

To a Long Loved Love: 4

You are still new, my love. I do not know you,
Stranger beside me in the dark of bed,
Dreaming the dreams I cannot ever enter,
Eyes closed in that unknown, familiar head.
Who are you, who have thrust and entered
My very being, penetrated so that now
I can never again be wholly separate,
Bound by shared living to this unknown thou?
I do not know you, nor do you know me,
And yet we know each other in the way
Of our primordial forbears in the garden,
Adam knew Eve. As we do, so did they.
They, we, forever strangers: Austere but true.
And yet I would not change it. You are still new.

To a Long Loved Love: 5

Words must be said, and silences be kept,
Yet, that word better left unheard, unspoken,
Like that unsaid, can wound. O Love, I've wept
From words, have thought my heart was broken
From the looked-for word unuttered. Where
Silence should speak loud, we speak instead.
Where words of love would heal we do not dare
To voice them: From sound and silence both have fled.
Yet love grows through those quiet deepening hours
When silence fills the empty boundless spaces
Twixt flesh and flesh. Wordlessness is ours
And love is nourished through unspoken graces.
But O my love, as I need daily bread
I need the words of love which must be said.

To a Long Loved Love: 6

Neither sadist nor masochist, I still
Must turn to violence: break, be broken.
False image of myself I beg you: kill.
Help me destroy the one of you I've spoken
Within my wilful heart. It is no more you
Than I am all that I would wish to be.
I cannot really love you till I hew
All these projections of an unreal me,
An imaged you, to shards. Then death
Will have a chance to free me for creation.
God! All this dying has me out of breath.
How do I understand reincarnation?
But if I burst all bonds of self-protection
Then may I find us both in resurrection.

To a Long Loved Love: 7

Because you're not what I would have you be
I blind myself to who, in truth, you are.
Seeking mirage where desert blooms, I mar
Your *you*. Aaah, I would like to see
Past all delusion to reality:
Then would I see God's image in your face,
His hand in yours, and in your eyes his grace.
Because I'm not what I would have me be,
I idolize Two who are not any place,
Not you, not me, and so we never touch.
Reality would burn. I do not like it much.
And yet in you, in me, I find a trace
Of love which struggles to break through
The hidden lovely truth of me, of you.

Epiphany

Unclench your fists
Hold out your hands.
Take mine.
Let us hold each other.
Thus is his Glory
Manifest.

Lovers Apart

In what, love, does fidelity consist?
I will be true to you, of course.
My body's needs I can resist,
Come back to you without remorse;

And you, behind the footlight's lure,
Kissing an actress on the stage,
Will leave her presence there, I'm sure,
As I my people on the page.

And yet—I love you, darling, yet
I sat with someone at a table
And gloried in our minds that met
As sometimes strangers' minds are able

To leap the bounds of times and spaces
And find, in sharing wine and bread
And light in one another's faces
And in the words that each has said

An intercourse so intimate
It shook me deeply, to the core.
I said good-night, for it was late;
We parted at my hotel door

And I went in, turned down the bed
And took my bath and thought of you
Leaving the theatre with light tread
And going off, as you should do,

To rest, relax, and eat and talk—
And I lie there and wonder who
Will wander with you as you walk
And what you both will say and do . . .

We may not love in emptiness;
We married in a peopled place;
The vows we made enrich and bless
The smile on every stranger's face,

And all the years that we have spent
Give me the joy that makes me able
To love and laugh with sacrament
Across a strange and distant table.

No matter where I am, you are,
We two are one and bread is broken
And laughter shared both near and far
Deepens the promises once spoken

And strengthens our fidelity
Although I cannot tell you how,
But I rejoice in mystery
And rest upon our marriage vow.

Lines After Herbert: Rondel

The contrarieties crush me. These crosse actions
Do winde a rope about, and cut my heart.
Good deeds are turned to sudden malefactions.
The end was never guessed at in the start.

How these stern contradictions break apart
The simplest words, and purest actions.
The contrarieties crush me: these crosse factions
Do winde a rope about and cut my heart.

A fearsome faith provides the only cautions.
O dear my Father, ease my smart.
Reality permits of no abstractions.
The whole is visioned in each broken part.
The contrarieties crush me: the crosse's actions
Do winde a rope about and hold my heart.

Epidaurus: The Theatre:
An Actor Muses

Truth is always masked,
is revealed, for mortals, only in signs.
With these magnificent flawed words
I reach for those harsh verities
which are past all the eager crowd
is willing to endure, truth being
neither charitable nor kind.
Behind the mask my face is distorted
by the dispassionate power
of the stern events I act, brutality of man,
inevitable punishment of fate
set in motion by the unconcerned
justice of the gods
who, being immortal,
are nonetheless concerned
with mortality,
dabble in it, consort with it,
to our destruction
and—perhaps—their shame.
With action and with words I reach
beyond the gods for that transcendent truth
which must, for us, be masked
or strike us dead.

The Animals Do Judge

Indica tigris agit rabida cum tigride pacem
Perpetuam: saevis inter se convenit ursis.
Ast homini ferrum letale incude nefanda
Produxisse parum est.

—Juvenal

We need not wait for God
The animals do judge
Of air and sea and grass
Accusing with their eyes
Waiting here en masse
They cry out with their blood
The whale caught in surprise
By oil slick's killing sludge
The cow with poisoned milk
The elephant's muted roar
At radioactive food
The tiger's mangy hide
The silkworm's broken silk
(The animals do judge)
The dead gulls on the shore
Mists of insecticide
Killing all spore and sperm
Eagle and owl have died
and nematode and worm
The snakes drag in the mud
Fallen the lion's pride

The night moth's wings are bruised
They cry out with their blood
Cain! Killer! We are named
By beast and bird condemned
By fish and fowl accused
We need not wait for God
The animals do judge.

The Guests of Abraham

I saw three angels seated at the table
Radiant and calm and wise and wholly real
As we, who stumble here, are quite unable
To be or know ourselves. If they will heal
Our broken bones, heal fish and meat
And bread and wine, heal wounds of mortal flesh,
Then may we take the lower seat
And join the throng, and side by side enmesh
The ill, the whole; the old, the young; and be
A single body, breaking fallen time,
A part of this creating Trinity,
Wiser than reason, lowly, and sublime.
I saw three angels standing at my door.
Come in! Come in! as you have done before.

Jacob: Ballade

Mortal and angel wrestle through the night,
Jacob struggling, wildly wondering why
An angel should choose man for this strange fight.
The crystal ladder breaks the fragile sky
As angels watch the two throughout the dark.
At dawn the angel smites tired Jacob's thigh;
Forever will he bear the wound and mark
God's messenger has left him. And the light
Of all the watching angels rises high;
The crystal ladder breaks the fragile sky.

The world is hushed and still; the earth is stark,
Astonished at the angel's choice and Jacob's cry.
Forever will he wear the wound and mark
The Lord has left to show his humble might.
All those who wrestle thus must surely die
To live once more to show the wound's strange sight.
The crystal ladder breaks the fragile sky
As angels rise and fall. The singing lark
Heralds the wild sun's brightly rising eye.
Forever will he bear the wound and mark.

Worn Jacob limps to show that God passed by;
(The crystal ladder breaks the fragile sky
And light shines bright within the glowing dark)
Forever will he bear the wound and mark.

David

Your altar smelled of the slaughter house.
The innocent eyes of tender beasts
Lost in confusions of laws and vows
Was the high price paid to you for feasts.
They had to be men of iron, your priests.

And so did I, born but to sing,
To tend the lambs and not to kill.
Why, my Lord, did you have to bring
Me down from the safety of my hill
Into the danger of your will?

I learned to fight, I learned to sin,
I battled heathen, fought with lust;
When you were on my side I'd win.
My appetites I could not trust.
I only knew your wrath was just.

What I desired I went and stole.
I had to fight against my son.
You bound my wounds and made me whole
Despite the wrong that I had done.
I turned from you and tried to run.

You took me, also, by the hair
And brought me back before your altar.
You terrified me with your care.
Against your rage I could but falter.
You changed me, but refused to alter.

So I grew old, but there remained
Within me still the singing boy.
I stripped and sang. My wife complained.
Yet all my ill did I destroy
Dancing before you in our joy.

My God, my God, is it not meet
That I should sing and shout and roar,
Leap to your ark with loving feet?
I praise thee, hallow, and adore,
And play before thee evermore.

Song from the Fiery Furnace

Mostly I burn.
The flames change not to dew.
To ashes turn
All who lose sight of you.

O holy three
Who danced amidst the fire
Come unto me:
The furnace blazes higher.

Flames purify.
Self's idol do not mourn
For it must die
That I to love be born.

Fire can't devour
The holy children's mirth
That turns this hour
From death to radiant birth.

O burning Son
Fiercer than furnace flame,
O purifying One,
Come, burn me with thy Name.

So, dead to sin,
Alive only in thee
My life begin
Now in eternity.

Annunciation

To the impossible: Yes!
Enter and penetrate
O Spirit. Come and bless
This hour: the star is late.
Only the absurdity of love
Can break the bonds of hate.

After Annunciation

This is the irrational season
When love blooms bright and wild.
Had Mary been filled with reason
There'd have been no room for the child.

Like Every Newborn

"The Lord is King, and hath put on glorious apparel;
the Lord hath put on his apparel,
and girded himself with strength:"

Like every newborn, he has come from very far.
His eyes are closed against the brilliance of the star.
So glorious is he, he goes to this immoderate length
To show his love for us, discarding power and strength.
Girded for war, humility his mighty dress,
He moves into the battle wholly weaponless.

The Risk of Birth, Christmas, 1973

This is no time for a child to be born,
With the earth betrayed by war & hate
And a comet slashing the sky to warn
That time runs out & the sun burns late.

That was no time for a child to be born,
In a land in the crushing grip of Rome;
Honour & truth were trampled by scorn—
Yet here did the Saviour make his home.

When is the time for love to be born?
The inn is full on the planet earth,
And by a comet the sky is torn—
Yet Love still takes the risk of birth.

. . . Set to the Music of the Spheres

Pain is a partner I did not request;
This is a dance I did not ask to join;
whirled in a waltz when I would stop and rest,
Jolted and jerked, I ache in bone and loin.
Pain strives to hold me close in his embrace;
If I resist and try to pull away
His grasp grows tighter; closer comes his face;
hotter his breath. If he is here to stay
Then must I learn to dance this painful dance,
Move to its rhythm, keep my lagging feet
In time with his. Thus have I a chance
To work with pain, and so may pain defeat.
Pain is my partner. If I dance with pain
Then may this wedlock be not loss but gain.

For M. S. J., 20th June, 1968

Madeleine Saunders Jones is here,
Sing joy, rejoice, and celebrate!
For perfect love doth cast out fear;
All heaven laughs to mark this date,
   Rejoice, rejoice,
   With merry voice,
A guardian angel takes his place
To help this darling grow in grace.

Rejoice, ye people of good will
And recompense ye with this love,
This proof that wild creation still
Can pain and death by joy remove.
   Take heed, take heed
   This loving deed
Gives lie to darkness and to death:
Creation blows this tiny breath.

Madeleine Saunders Jones has come!
Her rosy lips move: taste and see!
She makes this groping world her home;
She curls her fingers, sucks with glee,
   Is here, is here,
   Beloved and dear
To all she made to watch and wait.
Rejoice! Rejoice! and celebrate!

Charlotte Rebecca Jones,
22nd August, 1969

When the time comes it is always unexpected
And a miracle. Charlotte,
Caught in the violence of creation,
Thrust into life, disconnected
From her bearer, arrived, scarlet,
Shouting. There is no explanation

For the tearing violence of a birth.
The Lord himself, when the Word first was spoken,
Took fistfuls of formless chaos, wrested
Sky, sea, and our familiar earth
From naught. So nothingness by Love was broken
And it was good. And then God rested.

He calls his creatures each to take his part
In this great cosmic heave of love and birth,
Sharing the mighty act of his creation.
We understand this only with the heart,
With pain and joy and pure celestial mirth.
The miracle of Charlotte needs no explanation.

Charlotte

She explodes with joy.
Sparks of gold and diamond fly
from the tips of her fingers
and her dancing toes.
Her laugh is like a crystal ball
and yet it has the earthy healthiness
of blades of sun-ripe wheat.

When she implodes
with sorrow
she takes within her all the gold,
the diamonds and the sunny laughter.
Deep, deep within herself she goes
and hides the pain
protects it in her heart;
talks like an ordinary day
except the sun has gone
and the sky holds no blue.

Who knows
what thoughts she hides
from us and from herself?

She keeps her sorrow
and the scars
are underneath the flesh
unseen, enclosed within the shell.
The hidden grain of anguish
may one day turn
into a pearl.

Crosswicks

This house has known the poignant mirth
Of two centuries of living and dying;
Is, for us, the joyful place of birth,
Has held our infant, in his cradle lying;
Has known, under the weathered roof,
The noise of our four full generations,
Weaving laughter, and tears, in its warp and woof,
Demanding forbearance, love and patience;
Saw, this spring, a wedding, love's new breath,
Promises made with sober joy; then beheld
The long weeks of my mother's dying, and her death.
Birth, love, death, our house has held,
And this epiphany affirms the worth
Of hope and prayer, this time of all Love's birth.

God's Beast

Least important of all animals, I am a beast
of burden. I can carry heavy loads,
and I am more patient than a camel,
gentler of nature, though occasionally stubborn.
I am not considered intelligent,
and my name is used as an insult.

But when I see an angel in my path
I recognize a messenger of God.
"Stop!" the angel said to me, and I stopped,
obeying God rather than my master, Balaam,
who hit me and cursed me and did not see
the angel's brilliance barring our way.

Later, I took the path to Bethlehem,
bearing God's bearer on my weary back,
and stood beside her in the stable, trying to share
her pain and loneliness, and then the joy.

I carried on my back the Lord himself,
riding, triumphant, through Jerusalem,
But the blessings turned to curses,
Hosanna into Crucify him! Crucify him!

Least important of all animals, beast of burden,
my heaviest burden is to turn the curse into a blessing,
to see the angel in my path,
to bear forever the blessing of my Lord.

The Tenth Hour

Who is to comfort whom
in this time beyond comfort
this end of our time?
Can I, who already have one mother,
alive, oh, very alive, and not over-willing to share,
be another man's mother's son?
Perhaps if she could hold me, as she so small a time ago
    held him,
knowing him dead with only a fragment of her knowing,
the rest of herself, her arms, heart, lips,
not understanding death—
but we will not touch. Not that way.

Can she, who has lost in such a manner her son,
be mother once again, past child-bearing, caring,
to a man full grown?
I loved her son, ran from him, returned only for the end,
most miserable—I, not he—

"Son."

My lips move. "Mother." though no sound comes.
She leaves the hill, the three crosses.
I follow. To her empty house.
She does not weep or wail as I had feared.
She does the little, homely things, prepares a meal, then
O God
washes my feet.
"An angel came," she said,

"to tell me of his birth. And I obeyed.
No angel's come to tell me of his death."

This, I thought, was not an argument.
I held back tears, since she held hers, though foolishly.
We ate—somehow—she always listening.
I said, at last, "You do not mourn."
She looked down at me gravely.
"No, my son. My second given son.
I obeyed then. Shall I do less today?"

Pentecost

Whence comes this rush of wind?
I stand at the earth's rim
And feel it streaming by
My hair, my eyes, my lips.
I shall be blown clean off.
I cannot stand the cold.

Earth shrinks. The day recedes.
The stars rush in, their fire
Blown wild as they race by.
This wind's strange, harsh embrace
Holds me against the earth,
Batters me with its power.

My bones are turned to ice.
I am not here, nor there
But caught in this great breath.
Its rhythm cracks my ribs.
Blown out, I am expelled.
Breathed in, I am inspired.

The wind broods where it will
Across the water's face.
The flowing sea of sky
Moves to the wind's demand.

The stars stretch fiery tongues
Until this mortal frame

Is seared to bone, to ash,
And yet, newborn, it lives.

Joy blazes through the night.
Wind, water, fire, are light.

Corinth

We have been further flung in time than space,
span more centuries than miles of sea,
see Apollo and his chariot race
across a long-gone sky. Here we
tread where once Medea trod,
wild and mindless, as she raged
at faithlessness of man and god,
and jealousy was not assuaged
by the wanton ruthless death
of her own sons; her mother's hand
stopped their startled, unsuspecting breath.
She stood on these stones where we stand,
before that brilliant other sun
had risen in the broken sky
when bright Apollo's race was run,
his reins relinquished with a cry.
Too far we're flung through countless years
to feel the ancient gods' swift fall
or see compassion's painful tears
groove the stern cheeks of preaching Paul.

Ready for Silence

Then hear now the silence
He comes in the silence
in silence he enters
the womb of the bearer
in silence he goes to
the realm of the shadows
redeeming and shriving
in silence he moves from
the grave cloths, the dark tomb
in silence he rises
ascends to the glory
leaving his promise
leaving his comfort
leaving his silence

So come now, Lord Jesus
Come in your silence
breaking our noising
laughter of panic
breaking this earth's time
breaking us breaking us
quickly Lord Jesus
make no long tarrying
When will you come
and how will you come
and will we be ready
for silence
            your silence

Advent, 1971

When will he come
and how will he come
and will there be warnings
and will there be thunders
and rumbles of armies
coming before him
and banners and trumpets
When will he come
and how will he come
and will we be ready

O woe to you people
you sleep through the thunder
you heed not the warnings
the fires and the drownings
the earthquakes and stormings
and ignorant armies
and dark closing on you
the song birds are falling
the sea birds are dying
no fish now are leaping
the children are choking
in air not for breathing
the aged are gasping
with no one to tend them

a bright star has blazed forth
and no one has seen it
and no one has wakened

Come, Lord Jesus!

Come, Lord Jesus! Do I dare
Cry: Lord Jesus, quickly come!
Flash the lightning in the air,
Crash the thunder on my home!
Should I speak this aweful prayer?
Come, Lord Jesus, help me dare.

Come, Lord Jesus! You I call
To come (come soon!) are not the child
Who lay once in the manger stall,
Are not the infant meek and mild.
You come in judgment on our fall:
Help me to know you, whom I call.

Come, Lord Jesus! Come this night
With your purging and your power,
For the earth is dark with blight
And in sin we run and cower
Before the splendid, raging sight
Of the breaking of the night.

Come, my Lord! Our darkness end!
Break the bonds of time and space.
All the powers of evil rend
By the radiance of your face.
The laughing stars with joy attend:
Come, Lord Jesus! Be my end!

Come, Let Us Gather

After A. M. Allchin's article on R. S. Thomas

Come, let us gather round the table.
Light the candles. Steward, pour the wine.
It is dark outside. The streets are noisy
with the scurrying of rats, with shoddy
tarts, shills, thugs, harsh shouting.

And what comfort is cold within? We're able
to offer a slim repast. The taste of brine,
warm from fresh tears, is in the glass. Choosy
guests will not come here. The bread is body
broken. The wine is dark with blood. I'm doubting

if half of those invited will turn up.
Most will prefer a different table,
will go elsewhere with gentler foods to sup.
And yet this is indeed a wedding feast
and we rejoice to share the bitter cup,
the crumbs of bread. For O my Lord, not least
of all that makes us raise the glass, is that we toast
You, who assembled this uncomely group: our one
mysterious host.

At Communion

Whether I kneel or stand or sit in prayer
I am not caught in time nor held in space,
But, thrust beyond this posture, I am where
Time and eternity are face to face;
Infinity and space meet in this place
Where crossbar and upright hold the One
In agony and in all Love's embrace.
The power in helplessness which was begun
When all the brilliance of the flaming sun
Contained itself in the small confines of a child
Now comes to me in this strange action done
In mystery. Break time, break space, O wild
and lovely power. Break me: thus am I dead,
Am resurrected now in wine and bread.

Martha

Now
nobody can ever laugh at me again
I was the one who baked the bread
I pressed the grapes for wine.

Temper My Intemperance

Temper my intemperance, O Lord,
O hallowed, O adored,
My heart's creator, mighty, wild,
Temper Thy bewildered child.
Blaze my eye and blast my ear,
Let me never fear to fear
Nor forget what I have heard,
Even your voice, my Lord.
Even your Word.

Sonnet After Thomas

Thomas doubted: seeing, then believed;
Touched the wounded hands, the pierced side,
Knew once for all his Lord and God; received
The Word and taught it. While I, Lord, in my pride
Am shown your light and still trip over doubt,
Seeking in foolishness to understand
The infinite with my finite wit, am out,
Then, of my mortal mind; reject your hand
At the same moment that I hold it tight.
Knowing, I know not all the things I know;
Hearing, I hear not; seeing, seek the light;
Standing, fly skywards; running, am too slow.
  Here in captivity where my song is wrung
  Help me to find again my native tongue.

Love Letter

I hate you, God.
Love, Madeleine.

> I write my message on water
> and at bedtime I tiptoe upstairs
> and let it flow under your door.

When I am angry with you
I know that you are there
even if you do not answer my knock
even when your butler opens the door an inch
and flaps his thousand wings in annoyance
at such untoward interruption
and says that the master is not at home.

> I love you, Madeleine.
> Hate, God.

(This is how I treat my friends, he said to one great saint.
No wonder you have so few of them, Lord, she replied.)

> I cannot turn the other cheek
> It takes all the strength I have
> To keep my fist from hitting back
> the soldiers shot the baby
> the little boys trample the old woman
> the gutters are filled with groans
> while pleasure seekers knock each other down
> in order to get their tickets stamped first.

I'm turning in my ticket
and my letter of introduction.
You're supposed to do the knocking. Why do you burst
    my heart?

        How can I write you
        to tell you that I'm angry
        when I've been given the wrong address
        and I don't even know your real name?

I take hammer and nails
and tack my message on two crossed pieces of wood:

        Dear God
        is it too much to ask you
        to bother to be?
        Just show your hindquarters
        and let me hear you roar.

Love,
Madeleine

For Ascension Day, 1967

I know it's not like that sunny Sunday afternoon
When we went to the zoo; evening came too soon
And we were back on the crowded city street
Still full of pleasure from the afternoon's treat,
And our little girl clutched in her fingers a blue balloon.

It bobbed above our heads. Suddenly there came a cry,
A howl of absolute loss. We looked on high
And there we saw the balloon, ascending,
Turning and twirling higher and higher, blending
Into the smoky blue of the city sky.

We wiped the eyes, blew the little nose, consoled the tears,
Did not, of course, offer a new balloon, instead were silly,
        waggled our ears,
Turned sobs to laughter, accepted loss, and hurried
Home for dinner. This day is not like that. And yet they
        must have tarried,
Looking up into the sky the day he left them, full of loss
        and fears.

He had come back to them, was with them, and then was
        lost
Again, or so perhaps it seemed, the table left without the
        host.
The disciples did not understand all that he had said,
That comfort would be sent; there would be wine and
        bread.

Lost and abandoned (where is my blue balloon?) they did
    not comprehend until the day of Pentecost.
Even after he told them, his followers did not hear and
    see:
What is this that he saith unto us? A little while and ye
Shall not see me, and again a little while and ye shall. . . .
    when? tomorrow?
We do not understand. Lord, nor do I, and share thus in
    their sorrow.
At the same time that the Spirit sets my sorrow free
To turn to love, and teaches me through pain to know
That love will dwell in me, and I in love, only if I let
    love go.

After the Saturday Liturgy at Montfort

O taste, and see, how gracious the Lord is:
taste! taste and see
    bread, fresh and hot from the oven,
    spring water, bubbling up from the rocks on a hot day,
    tears, salt and warm as I kiss away a child's hurt,
    wine, shared, as the cup is passed,
    tears, salt and bitter, my tears, hot with pain,
    lips, tender and loving, comforting and healing,
O taste! taste and see.

O hear, and see, how gracious the Lord is:
hear! hear and see
    the thunder of his joy as galaxies fling across the
        Cosmos,
    the whisper of grass growing,
    the voice of the beloved,
    my own fingers finding the sound of Bach.
    the greeting of friends,
    laughter and sharing and song,
    and the words of healing bringing new life.
O hear! hear and see.

O sniff, smell and see, how gracious the Lord is:
smell! sniff and see
    the salt of the ocean and the rush of wind,
    the sweet puckering smell of grapes being pressed for
        wine,
    the odour of rising dough, promise of bread,

and oh, did you know you can recognize your own
    baby by its smell?
and those you love most dearly, too, the unique,
    original smell of flesh
created—like flaming suns, like the smallest hydrogen
    atom—
to the honour and glory of his Name
O sniff! smell and see.

O feel, and see, how gracious the Lord is:
Feel! touch and see
    bread in your fingers; feel it, bite and swallow;
    and wine, warm and living, spreading its fire through
        your body;
    take my hand, let me take yours, touch,
    so moves the Spirit through us—O touch me, heal me,
        hold me—
    God moves through our fingers—
    Reach out, touch the sun
    do not be afraid, O swallower of flame
    for this fire burns in order to give life.

Feel! Touch and see
    how gracious the Lord is!
Taste, hear, smell, feel, and see
    how gracious the Lord is!

Star Light

Perhaps
        after death
the strange timelessness, matterlessness,
   absolute differentness
        of eternity
will be shot through
like a starry night
with islands of familiar and beautiful
joys.

For I should like
to spend a star
sitting beside Grandpapa Bach
at the organ, learning, at last, to play
   the C minor fugue as he, essentially,
   heard it burst into creation;

and another star
   of moor and mist, and through the shadows
   the cold muzzle of the dog against my hand,
   and walk with Emily. We would not need to
   talk, nor ever go back to the damp of
   Haworth parsonage for tea.

I should like to eat a golden meal
   with my brothers Gregory and Basil,
   and my sister Macrina. We would raise
   our voices and laugh and be a little drunk
   with love and joy.

I should like a theatre star,
    and Will yelling, "No! No! that's not
    how I wrote it! but perhaps it's better
    that way: 'To be or not to be:' All
    right, then! Let it stand!"

And I should like
    another table
    —Yes, Plato, please come, and you, too,
    Socrates, for this is the essential table
    of which all other tables are only
    flickering shadows on the wall.
    This is the heavenly banquet,
    (Oh, come!)
    the eternal convivium.

The sky blazes with stars!

Ascension, 1969

Pride is heavy.
It weighs.
It is a fatness of spirit,
an overindulgence in self.
This gluttony is earthbound
Cannot be lifted up.
Help me to fast,
to lose this weight!
Otherwise, O Light One,
how can I rejoice in your
Ascension?

Sonnet, Trinity 18

Peace is the centre of the atom, the core
Of quiet within the storm. It is not
A cessation, a nothingness; more
The lightning in reverse is what
Reveals the light. It is the law that binds
The atom's structure, ordering the dance
Of proton and electron, and that finds
Within the midst of flame and wind, the glance
In the still eye of the vast hurricane.
Peace is not placidity: peace is
The power to endure the megatron of pain
With joy, the silent thunder of release,
The ordering of Love. Peace is the atom's start,
The primal image: God within the heart.

FROM *A CRY LIKE A BELL*

(1987)

Eve

When we left the garden we knew that it would be
        forever.
The new world we entered was dark and strange. Nights
        were cold.
We lay together for warmth, and because we were afraid
of the un-named animals, and of the others: we had never
known about the giants, and angels gone wild. We had
        not been told
of dwarves and elves; they teased us; we hid whenever they
        played.

Adam held me. When my belly grew taut and began to
        swell
I didn't know what was happening. I thought it was the
        beginning
of death, the very first death. I clung to Adam and cried.
As I grew bigger something within me moved. One day I
        fell
and the pains started. A true angel came and pushed the
        grinning
creatures back. Adam helped. There was a tearing. I
        thought I'd died.

Instead, from within me came a tiny thing, a new
        creature,
red-faced, bellowing, mouth groping for my breast.
This was not death, but birth, and joy came to my heart
        again.
This was the first-born child. How I did laugh and sing!

But from this birth came death. He never gave me any
  rest.
And then he killed his brother. Oh, my child. Oh, my son
  Cain.

I watched from then on over every birth,
seeing in each babe cruelty ready to kill compassion.
For centuries the pattern did not change. Birth always
  meant death.
Each manchild who was born upon the longing earth
in gratefulness and joy brought me only a fresh ration
of tears. I had let hate into the world with that first breath.

Yet something made me hope. Each baby born
brought me hurrying, bringing, as in the old tales, a gift
looking—for what? I went to every slum and cave and
  palace
seeking the mothers, thinking that at least I could warn
their hearts. Thus perhaps the balance might shift
and kindness and concern replace self-will and malice.

So I was waiting at that extraordinary intersection
of Eternity and Time when David's son (Adam's, too)
was born. I watched the Incarnate at his mother's breast
making, by his humble, holy birth the one possible
  correction
of all that I by disobedience had done. I knelt and saw
  new
Adam, and I cried, "My son!" and came at last to rest.

"And God heard . . ."

And God heard the voice of the lad [Ishmael];
and the angel of God called to Hagar out of heaven,
and said unto her, What aileth thee, Hagar?
Fear not; for God hath heard the voice of the lad where he
   is. . . .
And God opened her eyes, and she saw a fountain of water.

—Genesis 21:17, 19

Light
eye-thirsting for light
oh come
sight-drenching
night-wrenching
cloud-clearing
fountains of light
refreshing
renewing
caressing
blessing
star-flashing
love-revealing
dark blind-healing
day-dealing
eye-drenching
thirst-quenching
draughts of in-sight
in-light
eye

thy satellite
cloud-clearing
sun-searing
fear's flight
I
hearing
revering
adoring
thy
glory-splashing
light-crashing
Thee-light
O delight
O joy of thy
unextinguished
incomprehensible
glory of
light.

Sarah: Before Mount Moriah

Like a small mouse
I am being played with.
Pushed around, sent from home,
passed off as a sister,
free to be the sport of others
(nobody asked me).
Nobody asked if I wanted
to leave home and all my friends
(the cat never asks the mouse).
Would my womb have filled
if we had stayed where we were
instead of following strange promises?
My maid, giving my husband a child for me,
then made mock of me.
So when the angel came
announcing—promising—
a child in my womb long dry
what could I do but laugh?
And then warmth came again, and fullness,
and my child was born,
my laughter, my joy.

But do not play with me any more!
What kind of logic lurks in your promise
that the sky full of stars
is like the number of our descendents
and then demand the son's life who makes
that promise possible?

Can I trust a breaker of promises?
What kind of game is this?

Are you laughing at my pain
as I watch the child and his father
climb the mountain?
Am I no more than a mouse
to be played with?

I am a woman.
You—father-God—
have yet to learn
what it is to be a mother,

and so, perhaps, have I.
And if you give me back my laughter again,
then, together we can learn
and I will say—oh, I will sing!—
that you have regarded the lowliness
of your handmaiden.

Abraham: With Laughter

Unlike the other gods
you are not satisfied with holocausts
and the sweet smell of smoke.
Unlike the other gods
you do not let us be
but come and pitch your tent
with ours and sniff out
all we do. You are not satisfied
to have us satisfied,
to leave well enough alone.

No, you sent me out,
an old man, with your interfering
and your promises, and all your countings
of the stars and my son's son's sons.
You might have picked a better man
to fall before the terror of great darkness.
Twice, fear for my life
passed my wife off as sister.
Why not, with her barren womb?

And then a son. In my old age a son.
You do nothing like the other gods
and so I know you are my God
and my son's God and my son's sons'.
I do not understand the stars

uncountable in number;
nor do I understand you.

I wept. And when,
after all, you did not accept my sacrifice,
the ram brought laughter home.

The Ram: Caught in the Bush

Asked to leave Eden
where I, with all the other beasts,
remained after the two-legged creatures left,
I moved to the gates and the cherub
with the flaming sword
drew aside to let me by, wings folded across his eyes.

I trotted along a path through woods,
across a desert, made a long detour
around a lake, and finally climbed
a mountain, till
the trees gave way to bushes
and a rock.
An old man raised a knife.

He stood there by the rock
and wept and raised his knife.
So these are men, I thought,
and shook my head in horror, and was caught
within the springing branches of a bush.
Then there was lightning,
and the thunder came,
and a voice cried out to me:
O my son, my son,
slain before the foundation
of the world.
I felt the knife's edge.
For this I came from Eden,
for my will is ever his,

as I am his, and have life
in him, and he in me.
Thus the knife pierced his own heart.

And the old man laughed with joy.

Isaac

From now on, no fathers are to be trusted.
I know.
I felt the knife at my throat before the angel
stopped my father's hand.

How did it come to that?
The three day journey to Mount Moriah
   and the sharpened blade
   and I, laid on the stone slab,
   prepared for sacrifice?
I, the great gift of my parents' old age,
   so unexpected as to cause them laughter,
   and then, when the miracle came,
   to bring them laughter,
   to be laughter, Isaac, I—
What kind of God the Father would ask Abraham,
   Abraham, his son,
   to offer up Isaac, his son.
   Why ask?
   Why demand obedience for such a wanton sacrifice?
How can my father's Father be a God of love?
How could my father sharpen the knife?

No, fathers are not to be trusted.

And when my father's Father
   sent his Son up the mountain for an offering
   who, then, demanded such a sacrifice?
   Who was it he obeyed

who sent no angel
   and no ram?
Who was the father of my father's Father?

But, my father said, there is no Father's father.

Isaac: my very name means laughter,
   and I know only tears.

Would I laugh
if I could understand
that my father's Father
and the Son
and the ram caught by the horns
are one?

Esau

Wives I had already,
for no one (as usual) thought to guide me.
But my father, who gave my brother
the blessing which, like the birthright,
should have been mine,
told this favoured, cheating son
that the daughters of Canaan
were not good enough for him.
Ha! thought I, and went to Ishmael,
another first-born favoured by neither man nor God
and took his daughter to my wife and to my bed.

Mahaloth
who put a song in my heart
may God hear
and by my name
and the name of Mahaloth's father
and the well of water which God
gave him in the desert
I will sing my song to Mahaloth in
silence.

The world knows of Jacob's love
for Rachel,
and of God's love for Jacob
who took all which by birth was mine.
(My heel still hurts.)

But in Mahaloth
a fountain in the desert is mine
and a song in my heart
which God (if he wills)
may hear.

Rachel: At Joseph's Birth

First
before babe's birth
is death
death to safety
to the womb's wondrous warmth
death to dear darkness

danger
terror of tidal wave
a cruelty of light
an agony of air
a push of breath invading
listless lungs

Cry, sweet son, rage
at the indignity of birth
at death to safety
(and death of your mother's shame).

Be born, child,
into this brilliant, dangerous world
where love's piercing light
perfects darkness

where love's light
through all our deaths
shines us into birth.

Rachel: Birthing Benjamin

Fight the darkness. Fight.
Let night not rise.
Push the shadows back
with tearless eyes.
Fight the darkness. Bright
is the loving heart
pierced by the sword of light,
thrusting the darkness back.
Let night not rise.
Fight the darkness. Start
the fear-filled fight.
Love is the one surprise
that startles the dark.
Heed not the certain pain.
Hold anger back.
Push the shadows apart.
Dark's loss, light's gain,
fight the darkness, fight,
let it not rise.
Nor fear the pain.
Follow the light
which cannot be understood.
Oh break, my heart,
fight the darkness. Fight.
But O my God I would
push the shadows back
until I see the child.
Love is the one surprise.
I struggle toward the bright
joy that ends the night.

Benjamin's Birth

Birth and death
the opening of new life
the first tentative breath
followed by the unwelcome knife
of death.

I heard the cry
resentful and rebellious
of my newborn son
reluctant to emerge
from the safe darkness
of the womb
darker perhaps
and further from life
than the unknown terror
of the tomb.

In the dark waters, the child
knows nothing of Time—
knows nothing of the time
when he will be propelled
from the dark into light
when life will begin
with pain and terror
and the responsibility of breath.
Is it better never to know birth?
Better than the sharp
knowledge of death?

Leah

We lived by deceit,
all of us,
one no better than the other,
I as bad as the rest,
willing to take my sister's place
in Jacob's bed on her wedding night—
humiliated, but still willing.

How could it be that Jacob did not know?
After a wedding feast such as Laban
gave his son-to-be
how could it not be?
And I loved him,
his strange, smooth body,
and his strong and joyous play.
Out of my love I bore him children,
left off bearing,
and bore again,
still unloved by him.
And when he had her, too, to wife
his god, or ours, or both,
closed my sister's womb,
and then, incomprehensible,
re-opened it.

My father, keeping our Jacob with us
by deceit, by deceit
was himself cheated,
Jacob taking

the best of his beasts.
Until, surprised at Laban's anger, he stole us
and we fled. Deceitful still,
my sister stole our father's gods
and sat on them.

And yet, from our deceit
and from our love
we gave to Jacob
twelve sons, twelve nations
and, in the end,
one God.

Leah: The Unloved

Acceptance without hope is stark and cold,
slowing the warm beating of the heart
in a waterless desert. I am told
the teraphim will balance out each part:
"I gave you sons; I will not give you this;
this good I'll balance with this pain-filled evil.
After love's hope, another gets the kiss."
Laban's gods juggle—savage, and primeval.
My sons he loves; that is my only good.
Another hope is found in each hope's death.
Hope will not die; would that it could,
but back it comes with each expectant breath.
Unloved as I am, but love still tries to lift
acceptance into my heart's acceptable gift.

Jacob: After Rachel's Death

She lay between me and the sleeping skins,
her body white, pliant, mine
to enter, to be enclosed by her withinness.
She lay between me and the sleeping skins.

The baby fills the empty air with cries.
The ground is red with lost blood.

She lay between me and the blowing sand,
brought by the hot east wind
that stings the skin like insects.
We held each other in the embrace
of wind—I was in her and she held me
close
like no other woman.
She lay between me and the stinging sand.

The baby cries . . .

She lay between me and approaching death,
between me and my brother's anger,
between me and the angel's steel-soft wings.
Her softness was my strength,
her willingness my courage.
How will I face the angel?

It is I who must care now
for the child.

Pharaoh's Cross

It would be easier to be an atheist; it is the simple way out.
But each time I turn toward that wide and welcoming
        door
it slams in my face, and I—like my forbears—Adam,
        Eve—
am left outside the garden of reason and limited, chill
        science
and the arguments of intellect.
Who is this wild cherubim who whirls the flaming sword
'twixt the door to the house of atheism and me?

Sometimes in the groping dark of my not knowing
I am exhausted with the struggle to believe in you,
        O God.
Your ways are not our ways. Your ways are extraordinary.
You sent evil angels to the Egyptians and killed;
you killed countless babes in order that Pharaoh,
whose heart was hardened by *you* (that worries me, Lord)
might be slow to let the Hebrew children go.
You turned back the waters of the Red Sea
and your Chosen People went through on dry land
and the Egyptians were drowned, men with wives and
        children,
young men with mothers and fathers (your ways are not
        our ways)
and there was much rejoicing at all this death,
and the angels laughed and sang, and you stopped them,
        saying,
"How can you sing when my children are drowning?"

When your people reached Mount Sinai you warned
    Moses
not to let any of them near you lest you break forth
on them with death in your hand.
You are Love, and you command us to love,
and yet you yourself turn men's hearts to evil,
and you wipe out nations with one sweep of the hand—
the Amorites and the Hittites and the Peruzzites—
gone, all gone. It seems that any means will do, and yet—
all these things are but stories told about you by fallen
    man,
part of the story (for your ways are not our ways)
but not the whole story. You are our author,
and we try to listen and set down what you say,
but we suffer from faulty hearing and loss of language
and we get the words wrong.

Listen: you came to us as one of us
and lived with us and died for us and descended into hell
    for us
and burst out into life for us:

Do you now hold Pharaoh in your arms?

Moses

Where are you?
Are you?
Are you not-ness
Are you the terror of the loss of all senses
all sense
?

For us finite, fallen
spacebound, time enclosed beings—
it is not meet for us to come too close
(take off your sandals)
or try to comprehend
you
who are infinite
eternal, freely comprehending, comprehensive
therefore (if you will) beyond our rationality
demolishing all our reasonings
overturning all our fragile buildings
demolishing all structures where we look to see
you

and then you turn your back on us.

Perhaps
we come closest to you only thus
in your absence.
Put me in a cleft of the rock
protect me with your infinite hand
as the absolute silence

in the heart of the hurricane
shows me the sound of your footsteps.
And you, turning your back that I not be destroyed
may (if you will)
pass by.

Gershom: Son of Moses

Time and memory are rock under our feet.
But the rock journeys on,
higher than we, leading us
to the rock on which to build,
strangely giving wondrous water
for all our searing thirsts.

Time and memory are the rock
of ages breaking human time
sending down roots,
memories deeper than all our living
roots drinking the living waters
healing
blessing
redeeming all forgetfulness and folly
of time's trappings.

Time and memory are the rock
on which we stand and love and live
and know more than we know,
share more than we dare,
give more than we have
because the rock journeys us
toward wherever Love wills.

From the Lord's rock
comes radiant timeless joy.

Jepthah's Daughter

Does anybody hear me? El! Are you there?
Where are you? You said you would always care.
If you are not, then there is nothing anywhere.

I call, I cry, against my fate I batter.
Sharp in my ears the echoes fall and shatter.
My father's vow is final. Does it matter

he never thought he'd see me first? His word
is final. Lord, you who know each animal, each bird—
if I speak softly, will I then be heard?

No. Hush. I make no sound at all.
I wait in silence, still, in case you call.
All barriers of self and will must fall.

Take me beyond the grasp of nights and days.
Death leads me on to neither time, nor place.
Even in the dark can come El's grace.

Oh, God. Oh, El. The darkness, El, the cold
between the stars. There's nothing here to hold.

So am I dead? This endless silence roars
and flings me with the tide on golden shores.

Who is this man, here, eating fish, and bread?
How can I see and hear him, being dead?

He hands me broken bread and I am broken.
I do not understand the word that he has spoken.

But he is waiting for me, bright as a star.
"It's all right, child," he says. "You are. You *are*."

Jepthah's Daughter, 2

All the things that I must leave are good
because you made them. In those first new days
when nothing something was and stars were glad
and matter blazed into a song of praise
you saw what you had made and called it good.

So why must I turn now from all these things?
Take leave of taste and sound and scent and sight?
I do not understand such alterings,
my father's promise made to bring me night.
El, let me feel the touch of angels' wings!

Farewell, farewell, though you do not forget
you made and called them good, all these that I
must leave. In a fair fragrant garden plot
did we betray what you had done, so die
because we turned away and thus forgot?

So we forget again and yet again,
born with decay like marrow in our bones.
Is honorable death done for your gain?
How can we all be what we were once?
How can we wash away the mortal stain?

Farewell, O desert sand and burning sun,
farewell, O wondrous sound of wind and song,

farewell, O living taste of bread and wine,
and touch of hand to hand within the throng.
Farewell to all that I have thought was mine.

Farewell to everything I thought was me
that I may know what these were meant to be.

Naaman, the Leper

O all ye little gods of Baal
whose altars crown the highest places,
at whom I scream to no avail,
who greet me with a thousand faces

their promises false—these alien priests.
My stricken skin's a leper's still.
I gave them jewels, spread them feasts,
and yet they never have their fill.

O all ye little gods of Baal,
first I must call you each by name;
and hunt each one through hill and dale
who spread abroad their worthless claim.

O all ye little gods of fear,
in alien dark, in the unknown,
gods of the soft, self-pitying tear,
gods of the self-willed need to own,

O all ye golden gods of pride,
ye whining gods of sly self-will,
in the high places you abide
and I must come and hunt and kill.

Where are your priests to feel my sword?
Come, you seducers, come you all,
beneath the double-edged word
clay feet shall shatter, heads shall fall.

Ye gods of jealousy and greed,
of lazy lust, of tired minds bored,
of cold, hard hearts. How fast you breed
to keep me from the only Lord.

O gods who tempted my false pride.
That seven washings in the river
were far too easy! "Master, bide,
obey the prophet." Healed flesh does quiver.

O all ye little gods of Baal
in the high places of the land
if I should hunt you down and fail
Elijah's here to guide my hand.

David: From Psalm 32

Teach me to obey willingly,
turning at the word of your command.
Under strong touch of your hand,
help to obey lovingly,
not questioning the turn in the road,
needing neither spur nor goad,
following your word joyfully.

Lend me, Lord, your understanding
not like horse or stubborn mule
balking against your rule
without the whip of your commanding.

Merrily, Lord, help me to play,
ride me without bit or bridle,
ride me bareback, without saddle,
ride me, move me to obey.

David: After Psalm 49

Death my shepherd
my loneliness
leading me through dark pastures
into unknown, unknowable emptiness
death my shepherd
the other side of light
the no of God
death the Son
thy sun
beyond all consolation
past human touch
death my loneliness
aloneness
teach me this dark lyric for my harp
that I may sing.

Psalm 55:12–14: A Contemplation of David

My heart is disquieted within me, and the fear of death
has fallen upon me, death of hope,
death of love, death of light,
for it is not an open enemy who has done me this
      dishonour,
for then I could have borne it;
(dark from dark is never a surprise;
hate where there is always hate is bitter, but bearable)
but it was thou, my guide, my old familiar friend,
who taught me the way, who kept my candle alight
(Were you only playing with matches?).
We took sweet counsel together,
and walked in this house of God as friends.
Then suddenly your words rained fire
and I could not escape the stormy wind and tempest.
Oh, my friend, you had hands and held me,
you had eyes and saw me; ears and heard me;
you had a mouth and spoke gently to me,
but now all I see is a painted wooden idol,
blind and deaf and dumb and unincarnate.
(Was it I who daubed flesh and blood
to this thing of clay?)

I brought you a cup of water; you dashed it to the floor.
I am emptied, and cold.

Sand stretches before me, and the desert is dark;
for company I find only my bare and broken bones.
My tears are my meat day and night.

O Light of the world, how do I rejoice?

Herman the Ezragite: Psalm 88:18

My lovers and friends hast thou put away from me,
and hid mine acquaintance out of my sight.

My friends are taken, and my love:
my heart is shaken,
   I move in loneliness into the cold,
hoarfrost beneath, ice stars above.
   My heart grows still: so grow I old.

Groping with empty hands I vow
soliloquies I'll not allow
   in this strange, frozen solitude
lest I should with weak tears endow
   the winter's breath, black, bleak, and rude.

The panic clang of closing doors
slams noisily into my prayers.
   I see the shut doors of the past,
their faces blank (tell me: who cares?).
   The future's doors are slamming fast.

If I should cry or weep or moan
I make myself the more alone.
   By laughter, only, and by jest
this fearfulness may be undone
   and I in loneliness find rest.

In doorless places I must go
step barefoot through the falling snow,
    followed or following, must not flee.
I cannot know nor seek to know
    where the next open place will be.

Annunciation

1

Sorrowfully
the angel appeared
before the young woman
feared
to ask what must be asked,
a task
almost too great to bear.
With care,
mournfully,
the angel bare
the tidings of great joy,
and then
great grief.
Behold, thou shalt conceive.
Thou shalt bring forth a son.
This must be done.
There will be no reprieve.

2

Another boy
born of woman (who shall also grieve)
full of grace
and innocence
and no offence—
a lovely one
of pure and unmarked face.

3

How much can a woman bear?

4

Pain will endure for a night
but joy comes in the morning.

His name is Judas.

That the prophets may be fulfilled
he must play his part.
It must be done.
Pain will endure.
Joy comes in the morning.

Bearer of Love

The great swan's wings were wild as he flew down;
Leda was almost smothered in his embrace.
His crimson beak slashed fiercely at her gown—
lust deepened by the terror on her face.

Semele saw her lover as a god.
Her rash desire was blatant, undenied.
He showed himself, thunder and lightning shod.
Her human eyes were blasted and she died.

And Mary sat, unknowing, unaware.
The angel's wings were wilder than the swan
as God broke through the shining, waiting air,
gave her the lily's sword thrust and was gone.

The swans, the old gods fall in consternation
at the fierce coming of the wild wind's thrust
entering Mary in pure penetration.
The old gods die now, crumbled stone and rust.

Young Mary, moved by Gabriel, acquiesced,
asked nothing for herself in lowliness,
accepted, too, the pain, and then, most blest,
became the bearer of all holiness.

The Bethlehem Explosion

And it came to pass in those days,
that there went out a decree from Caesar Augustus,
that all the world should be taxed. . . .
And Joseph also went up from Galilee . . . to be taxed
with Mary his espoused wife, being great with child.

                                        —*Luke 2:1, 4–5*

The chemistry lab at school
was in an old greenhouse
surrounded by ancient live oaks
garnished with Spanish moss.

The experiment I remember best
was pouring a quart of clear fluid
into a glass jar, and dropping into it,
grain by grain, salt-sized crystals,
until they layered
like white sand on the floor of the jar.

One more grain—and suddenly—
water and crystal burst
into a living, moving pattern,
a silent, quietly violent explosion.
The teacher told us that only when
we supersaturated the solution,
would come the precipitation.

The little town
was like the glass jar in our lab.
One by one they came, grain by grain,
all those of the house of David,
like grains of sand to be counted.

The inn was full. When Joseph knocked,
his wife was already in labour; there was no room
even for compassion. Until the barn was offered.
That was the precipitating factor. A child was born,
and the pattern changed forever, the cosmos
shaken with that silent explosion.

Young Mary

I know not all of that which I contain.
I'm small; I'm young; I fear the pain.
All is surprise: I am to be a mother.
That Holy Thing within me and no other
is Heaven's King whose lovely Love will reign.
My pain, his gaining my eternal gain
my fragile body holds Creation's Light;
its smallness shelters God's unbounded might.
The angel came and gave, did not explain.
I know not all of that which I contain.

Three Songs of Mary

1. *O Simplicitas*

An angel came to me
and I was unprepared
to be what God was using.
Mother I was to be.
A moment I despaired,
thought briefly of refusing.
The angel knew I heard.
According to God's Word
I bowed to this strange choosing.

A palace should have been
the birthplace of a king
(I had no way of knowing).
We went to Bethlehem;
it was so strange a thing.
The wind was cold, and blowing,
my cloak was old, and thin.
They turned us from the inn;
the town was overflowing.

God's Word, a child so small
who still must learn to speak
lay in humiliation.
Joseph stood, strong and tall.
The beasts were warm and meek
and moved with hesitation.
The Child born in a stall?

I understood it: all
Kings come in adoration.

Perhaps it was absurd;
a stable set apart,
the sleepy cattle lowing;
and the incarnate Word
resting against my heart.
My joy was overflowing.
The shepherds came, adored
the folly of the Lord,
wiser than all men's knowing.

2. *O Oriens*

O come, O come Emmanuel
within this fragile vessel here to dwell.
O Child conceived by heaven's power
give me thy strength: it is the hour.

O come, thou Wisdom from on high;
like any babe at life you cry;
for me, like any mother, birth
was hard, O light of earth.

O come, O come, thou Lord of might,
whose birth came hastily at night,
born in a stable, in blood and pain
is this the king who comes to reign?

O come, thou Rod of Jesse's stem,
the stars will be thy diadem.

How can the infinite finite be?
Why choose, child, to be born of me?

O come, thou key of David, come,
open the door to my heart-home.
I cannot love thee as a king—
so fragile and so small a thing.

O come, thou Day-spring from on high:
I saw the signs that marked the sky.
I heard the beat of angels' wings
I saw the shepherds and the kings.

O come, Desire of nations, be
simply a human child to me.
Let me not weep that you are born.
The night is gone. Now gleams the morn.

Rejoice, rejoice, Emmanuel,
God's Son, God's Self, with us to dwell.

3. *O Sapientia*

It was from Joseph first I learned
of love. Like me he was dismayed.
How easily he could have turned
me from his house; but, unafraid,
he put me not away from him
(O God-sent angel, pray for him).
Thus through his love was Love obeyed.

The Child's first cry came like a bell:
God's Word aloud, God's Word in deed.
The angel spoke: so it befell,
and Joseph with me in my need.
O Child whose father came from heaven,
to you another gift was given,
your earthly father chosen well.

With Joseph I was always warmed
and cherished. Even in the stable
I knew that I would not be harmed.
And, though above the angels swarmed,
man's love it was that made me able
to bear God's love, wild, formidable,
to bear God's will, through me performed.

O Wise and Foolish Virgins

Her rounded belly moved with life.
He felt it with his calloused hands
the pain slashed through her like a knife.
She fell, gave way to birth's demands,
    and in her pain
    delivered Cain.
New life within her body grew.
Trembling, he led her to the stall
and quivered as the pain knifed through.
He thought he heard an angel call.
    Her flesh was torn—
    Jesus was born.

Now we await the final birth.
The oil has spilled. No one is wise.
The galaxies and our small earth
labour in pain at time's demise.
    Like her, I call,
    Come, Lord of all!

First Coming

He did not wait till the world was ready,
till men and nations were at peace.
He came when the Heavens were unsteady,
and prisoners cried out for release.

He did not wait for the perfect time.
He came when the need was deep and great.
He dined with sinners in all their grime,
turned water into wine. He did not wait

till hearts were pure. In joy he came
to a tarnished world of sin and doubt.
To a world like ours, of anguished shame
he came, and his Light would not go out.

He came to a world which did not mesh,
to heal its tangles, shield its scorn.
In the mystery of the Word made Flesh
the Maker of the stars was born.

We cannot wait till the world is sane
to raise our songs with joyful voice,
for to share our grief, to touch our pain,
He came with Love: Rejoice! Rejoice!

The Wise Men

A star has streaked the sky.
pulls us,
calls.
Where, oh where, where leads the light?

We came and left our gifts
and turned
homeward.
Time had passed, friends gone from sight—

One by one, they go, they die
to now,
to us—
gone in the dazzling dark of night.

Oh how, and where, and when, and why,
and what,
and who,
and may, and should, O God, and might

a star, a wind, a laugh, a cry
still come
from one—
the blazing word of power and might—

to use our gifts of gold and myrrh
and frankincense
as needed,
as our intention was to do the right?

Here, there, hear—soft as a sigh—
willing,
loving
all that is spoken, back to the flight

blazing too fierce for mortal eye.
Renew—
redeem,
oh, Love, until we, too, may dazzle bright.

One King's Epiphany

I shall miss the stars.

Not that I shall stop looking
as they pattern their wild wills each night
across an inchoate sky, but I must see them with a
    different awe.
If I trace their flames' ascending and descending—
relationships and correspondences—
then I deny what they have just revealed.
The sum of their oppositions, juxtapositions,
led me to the end of all sums:
a long journey, cold, dark and uncertain,
toward the ultimate equation.
How can I understand? If I turn back from this,
compelled to seek all answers in the stars,
then this—Who—they have led me to
is not the One they said: they will have lied.
No stars are liars!
My life on their truth!
If they had lied about this
I could never trust their power again.

But I believe they showed the truth,
truth breathing,
truth Whom I have touched with my own hands,
worshipped with my gifts.
If I have bowed, made
obeisance to this final arithmetic,
I cannot ask the future from the stars without betraying

the One whom they have led me to.
It will be hard not to ask, just once again,
to see by mathematical forecast where he will grow,
where go, what kingdom conquer, what crown wear.
But would it not be going beyond truth
(the obscene *reductio ad absurdum*)
to lose my faith in truth once, and once for all
revealed in the full dayspring of the sun?

I cannot go back to night.
O Truth, O small and unexpected thing,
You have taken so much from me.
How can I bear wisdom's pain?
But I have been shown: and I have seen.

Yes. I shall miss the stars.

". . . and kill the Passover"

. . . and kill the Passover.

—Exodus 12:21

Angel! Messenger of light and death—
Is it by God's will that you have come?
Each year I gave thanks and rejoiced
that the blood of the lamb was on the lintel
and you passed over the homes of Israel,
God's children, and did not put your cold hand
upon our first born babes. It was only those Egyptians,
the babes of those who worshipped foreign gods—
or no gods at all—that you struck down.
I did not even notice
the mourning of those Egyptian mothers.
Was not this God's doing, and for our sakes,
that our people might go free of bondage?
Our mothers held their living infants
to their breasts; perhaps they laughed with joy.
Our God had once more saved his Chosen People.

God!
Was not my slaughtered baby chosen, too?
Who is this child whose stabled birth
caused Herod's panic and revenge? Lord!
Every Hebrew manchild under two, clubbed, stabbed,
    killed.
Who was your angel, then? Angel of light and death—
was it God's sword that flashed against our babes?

How can I ever again rejoice at Passover,
when other women's babes, innocent of all guile,
were slaughtered by your angel?
Passover—and where's my child—
my Herod-hated, slaughtered, butchered babe?
Your ways are not our ways, O God of love.
I do not understand the evil angels sent
among Egyptians, nor the mothers,
bereaved as Rachel, weeping for their dead.
I hold the bloody body of my babe and curse you
that you did not stay the cruel sword.
Is this your love, that all these die
that one star-heralded man-child should live?
And what will be his end, O Lord? How will he die?
How will you show this one saved child your love?

Mary: After the Baptism

Yes, of course. On many days I doubted.
My faith grew out of doubt. The child was good
but other babies have been good. He shouted
when he was hungry, like any child, for food.
One simply does not think of the Messiah
cutting teeth, eating, and eliminating.
He springs, full-grown, in the great Isaiah—
God, servant, king. And I was waiting,
remembering in my heart the very things
that caused my doubt: the angel's first appearing
to me and then to Joseph; shepherds, kings,
the flight to Egypt. Remembering was fearing;
doubt helped. I had to face it all as true
the day John baptized him. Then he knew.

The Preparation of Mary, Mother of Joses

Neither virgin nor wise
I fill foolishly
my lamp, lest surprise
take me unprepared. Mulishly
at mid-morning sun-time
I pour in the oil.
(I'm anticipating as usual.)
Toil is my lot,
my daily drink and meat.
The Bridegroom will find me workworn and rough.
But my lamp is ready, and even as I am,
I'll gladly greet Him who comes.
And that is joy enough.

Andrew

Jesus, too, needed friends; close friends
and solitude. The companionable meal,
laughter and talk—then he, the one who spends
himself must turn himself, turn, and conceal
himself in desert emptiness to be
by Father filled. And then poured strength upon
all the emptiest, the most in need. And he,
being human for us, needed me, Peter and John.
So taught he us. So did we learn
this lovely rhythm—needing, needed—then
the deepest of all needs, the heartward turn
to Love's own source, the spring which fills all men,
Son-lit, Father-filled, Spirit-blown.
By yourself, Lord, to us our self is shown.

The Samaritan Woman at the Well

The waters are wild, are wild.
Billows batter with unchannelled might.
A turmoil of waves foams on the ocean's face
wind-whipped the waters hurl

the rivers rush

fountains burst from the rocks
the rapids break huge boulders into dust
the skies split with torrential rains

waters meet waters
the wind and waves are too tumultuous
no one can meet them and survive

In this wilderness of water
we shall all be drowned
the ocean cannot be compassed

I weep, I die
Put my tears in your bottle

drowning
I thirst

Look!
the water is in a cup

(O Lord open thou our lips)

I thirst

Is it any less water
because you have contained it for us
in a vessel we can touch?

Song of Blind Bartimaeus After His Healing

All praise to thee, my God, this night
for all I see, both night and day.
All praise for loveliness of things!

During the shadows of un-sight
you kept the raging fears at bay.
All praise to thee, my God, this night

for all the blessings of the light,
for sand and sun and eagles' wings,
all praise for loveliness of things!

Praise for sandals, garments white,
for children's faces, eyes alight,
all praise to thee, my God, this night.

All praise for butterflies in flight,
for work-worn hands, for golden hay,
the purple shadows evening brings,

for brass and copper polished bright,
for lifting light that shows the way,
all praise to thee, my God, this night,
all praise for loveliness of things!

The Woman

Jesus, to the woman taken in adultery:
Go, and sin no more.

It is not
what it was
or could have been
or might have been
or should have been
or what I thought it would be
or dreamed about
or expected
or longed for
or prayed for.

It is what is.
Nowhere else but
Here. Now.
Only in the is
(not the ought)
does love grow—
is joy found.

Never in vain hopings
in vanity
in vaunting
or wishing or pretending
or dreaming
but here. Now.

Never in saying
it was not my fault
it shouldn't have been
I couldn't help it
but I meant
but he didn't
but you don't understand.

Never
there.
Only here
in the painful light
of my own sin
accepted
seen in its ugliness
repented
forgiven
(forgiveness hurts)

let me turn
seeking nothing
asking nothing
here
only here
is the longed for
Word.

Only now can I say
I love you.

"When Mary asked . . ."

When Mary asked for him . . . Jesus said,
"Who is my mother? and who are my brethren?"

—*Matthew 12:46, 48*

He heals, my son, he heals the blind,
the lepers, and those possessed of unclean spirits.
When his hands touch, no wound is mortal.
But we can still die. Day
can be held back by night's uncomprehending portal.

I bleed. I faint. I die.
(A sword will pierce you, Simeon said.)
Nothing is automatic, nothing is guaranteed.
Love is not killed although my heart may cry
as the sword pierces. Love may not heed

betrayal or rejection, being
of its essence impossible, like everything essential.
While love is dying it is being reborn. Seeing
its own mortal wound it is of confidential

opinion that these are pains of labour.
During love's delivery I am ripped and torn.
Who, my son asks, who is your neighbour?
Son, all that matters is that love is born.

The High Priest's Servant

Sometimes I take it out and look at it
(unrecognizable now
unless one knew it full of blood and sound)
shrivelled like an old heel of bread,
or piece of fungus.

I was certainly not prepared.
I knew my master had it in for
some itinerant preacher,
and it seemed to me that his high priest's fear and anger
exceeded anything this Galilean might do.
But my master was always given to extremes,
and what could I do but go along
with him and the others
on that warm, crucial night?

It would have been simpler
to take the man by day (though less dramatic).
We came to the agreed-on place,
where an ill-named friend approached to kiss him
so we'd be certain we had the right man.
After a sudden flurry of torches and shouting
a stunning pain slashed down my head.
The roar of anguish within me
was louder than my scream.

And then he touched me, this strange man we'd trapped,
and the intolerable roaring cleared,
and I heard the small song of a night bird,

and the wind moving in the olive trees
beyond the heavy breathing of frightened men.

I bent down and picked it up.
Then lifted my hands,
felt my head, and two ears, warm and hearing.

And my life was shattered, turned around,
and changed forever. I left the high priest,
never to return.

There is danger now.
Often we do not understand
our freedom, and the fresh blood flowing in our lives.
That is why I sometimes take it out and look at it,
unrecognizable now,
unless one knew it full of song and sound.

Andrew: Having Run Away from Jesus in the Garden

Who is this stranger whom I hardly know,
(despite his presence within me) who cannot
be kept decently silent and unseen
(Lord, I still feel my muscles, tight from running),
with whom I must be reconciled
before I can sleep? This unwelcome
intruder who is my self
must be forgiven and accepted
and somehow loved. You have forgiven me,
with your unexpected presence among us.
But even in my joy I know I betrayed you
and must forever know that this coward, too,
is as much me as the loyal disciple I thought to be.

This stranger who is most of me is still
my Lord's failed friend, but friend nevertheless,
and in this friend I now must find, before I sleep,
His image, and His love.

Magdalen

I sold that which is forever and unspeakably priceless.
I was paid for that which can only be given away.
Asked for my reasons I stood, strangely struck voiceless.
A cloud unexpectedly darkened the brilliant day.

I turned from the cushions. the perfumes, the endless
      lying.
Hunger meant nothing; I was replete at last.
I think I was born, yet I know that this is dying.
I eat of the feast as I turn away for the fast.

In fear, in joy, I lose myself in the finding.
The lusts of the body are shriven, the flesh is new.
Fresh grave cloths are all my selfish self is binding.
Lord! This is my body which I would give for you.

Mary of Magdala

How do I find You, who have been blinded by the
    brilliance of your Father?
The darkness is heavy in tangible weight.
Am I afraid of light? Would I rather
remain in the shadows, afraid of the brightness of your
    face?
Why must I stay here where the black clouds gather,
trying to slow the hours in this dim place,
to halt time's vast, inexorable race.

How do I find You? Through what graces?
Why am I frightened by the height of this wild, windy
    day
I who have always passionately loved light?
Why do I see you in the darkest places,
touch your garment only when I turn away?
Or see your radiance when ugliness and grief
seem to leave no room for you to stay?
I see you in distorted, hungry faces.
In crusts and filthy gutters is belief
in your love breaking all hate.
You have left your traces
on this demoniac's freed face and joy-streaked cheek.

I find you, Lord, when I no longer clutch.
I find you when I learn to let you go,
and then you reach out with your healing touch.
Seven demons left my tortured mind!
My Lord, so stern, so infinitely kind,
I know myself at last because *you* know.

Simon of Cyrene

I've rolled too many stones—nay, boulders—
up this never-ending hill, pushing my shoulders
against the heavy, jagged chunk of granite,
crying against the weight of the entire planet,
staggering like one condemned, up, up the mountain,
the long road dusty, never a spring or fountain,
pushing this boulder which grows heavier steadily,
the Eumenides at my heels, implacable, deadly.
If I near the top, the rock's at the bottom again.
There's no end to labour, climbing, struggle, pain.

Who do you think you are, carrying another man's stone?
Sisyphus is gone long since; the old gods gone.
Other men's burdens are not your burden unless
they're offered you freely, never under duress.
What you must carry was long ago prepared
before the morning stars sang and the worlds were shared.
Its weight is infinite; yet you will find it light.
It will bow your back, and yet you must walk upright.
The hill is endless, but you will reach its peak.
The strong will falter; help will come from the weak.
When you have reached the place where others before you
    have stood,
you will find that your burden is made not of stone, but of
    wood.

Barabbas

Son of man
Son of the Father—
who can
tell one from the other?
Son of man
must taste of death.
Father's son,
I would rather
be the one
to return
to Father's side
than to remain
to mourn
man's son's pain.
So he died
while my breath
burned in the rain.

Son of man
dead for me,
crucified,
to set me free.
Son of the Father,
I must be
because my brother
toppled death
upon a tree.

The cross's death
becomes life's door.

Son of man
offers more
abundant life
than those whose scorn
had thought to kill
the coming morn.

Son of man
my life will turn,
as to our Father
I return.

Mary Speaks:

O you who bear the pain of the whole earth,
    I bore you.
O you whose tears give human tears their worth,
    I laughed with you.
You, who, when your hem is touched, give power,
    I nourished you.
Who turn the day to night in this dark hour,
    light comes from you.
O you who hold the world in your embrace,
    I carried you.
Whose arms encircled the world with your grace,
    I once held you.
O you who laughed and ate and walked the shore,
    I played with you.
And I, who with all others, you died for,
    now I hold you.

May I be faithful to this final test:
in this last time I hold my child, my son,
his body close enfolded to my breast,
the holder held: the bearer borne.
Mourning to joy: darkness to morn.
Open, my arms: your work is done.

Salome: At the Foot of the Cross

Mark 15:40

It is the crossbeam with its earthbound weight,
that hurts, that makes his uphill road unending.
At the summit the upright waits, uncompromising,
    unbending.
He will have unthinkable pain, perhaps no angels
    tending,
so solitary is the road, so strait the gate.

Does this road go uphill only?
Is death all that waits at the end?

Under the cross I sit and, time-bound, wait
for time to fit the crossbeam to the upright, knowing
the end. He staggers, he is here, his weakness growing.
Flesh and wood shudder under the icy blowing.
Oh, Lord, is this how all our hopes must end?

Pushing through dark, in fiercest concentration,
it is now, as he stands beneath the crossbeam's weight
that he strengthens, stretches, now he carries nothing,
it would seem, except himself. It is too late
for me to bear it for him, carry his beam,
and not the beam in my own eye, blinding, blowing.
Oh, God, the hammer, the nails. Lord.
He is stretched out, his strong arms

nailed to the crossbeam,
his dust-darkened feet to the upright.

Is there only time, this sky-darkened time?
As night dies to morning,
will his dawn ever break again?

Three Days

Friday:

When you agree to be the mother of God
you make no conditions, no stipulations.
You flinch before neither cruel thorn nor rod.
You accept the tears; you endure the tribulations.

But, my God, I didn't know it would be like this.
I didn't ask for a child so different from others.
I wanted only the ordinary bliss,
to be the most mundane of mothers.

Saturday:

When I first saw the mystery of the Word
made flesh I never thought that in his side
I'd see the callous wound of Roman sword
piercing my heart on the hill where he died.

How can the Word be silenced? Where has it gone?
Where are the angel voices that sang at his birth?
My frail heart falters. I need the light of the Son.
What is this darkness over the face of the earth?

Sunday:

Dear God, He has come, the Word has come again.
There is no terror left in silence, in clouds, in gloom.

He has conquered the hate; he has overcome the pain.
Where, days ago, was death lies only an empty tomb.

The secret should have come to me with his birth,
when glory shone through darkness, peace through strife.
For every birth follows a kind of death,
and only after pain comes life.

Pieta

The other Marys radiated joy.
The disciples found the truth hard to believe.
There had to be breaking bread, eating fish,
before they, too, even Thomas, were lit with joyfulness.

Not much was said about me.
I said good-bye to the son I carried within me
for nine months, nursed, fed, taught to walk.
On Friday when they took him down from the cross,
I held the son I knew,
recognizing him in my arms,
and never saw him again,
not my body's child.

How could I laugh, weep tears of joy?
Like the others, I failed to recognize him;
the Christ who rose was not Bethlehem's babe.
And it was right. For this was meant to be.
Here in my head I would not have had it otherwise.
But empty arms still longed for familiar flesh.
My joy, a sword that pierced through my heart.

I understood, more, perhaps, than the others
when he said that he could not stay with us—
that it was better if he went away,
was one again with God, his Father.
And when the Spirit came
I once again could love my son
and know my Lord.

If Easter came later for me than for the others,
its brilliance was as poignant and bright.

Mary: Afterwards

John. John, can you not take me to him,
you who were more than friend, who are now my son?
After all we have known and borne together
can you deny to me now that you've surely seen him?
Can you conceal his whereabouts from his mother?
I ran to the place where the other Marys knew him;
I saw the empty tomb, the enormous stone
rolled from its mouth, the grave clothes lying.
I called, I cried, with no one there to hear me.
Joy and grief raged in my longing heart.
He was not there, nor even the flaming angel.
I was the last to be told. Why were you all
afraid to say what I most wanted to hear?
I know: the Magdalen said that she couldn't touch him,
that she knew him only because he called her: Mary!
On the Emmaus road they didn't know they'd been
        walking
beside him until he was known in the breaking of bread.
John, do you fear that perhaps I wouldn't know him?
Perhaps it would give me pain to find my son
so changed from the son I knew, the son I circled
first with my body, last with my anguished arms.

John: I can bear to know that I may not hold him.
The angel who came to me once will help me now.
I don't need to touch him. Just let me see him . . .
Don't be impatient: "Mother, you don't understand!"
I've never pretended, my dear, to understand him.
Only to love him, to be there if ever he needed

to know I was by him, waiting and loving—
Oh, John. Yes. I see. That's how it will be, then?
You don't know where he is? You're alone, and then
he's with you, but it's different now.
He comes, and he's gone, and you know him
only by what he says or what he does,
by his hands and feet, or in the breaking of bread.
The angel told me before his birth, and Simeon
after, and I haven't ever asked more—or less.
If my joy in him must rest only in your witness
that he is risen, that he is risen indeed,
then he has given you to me to help me bear it.
We have shared the cup, and the dark of night is done.
I will know my son through you he has given me for my
      son.

Thomas: After Seeing the Wounds

As you depended from a tree,
so depend I, Lord, on thee.
Thou my cross; on thee impaled
is my body. Now I see
how our hands and feet are nailed,

nailed by joy and nailed by pain:
strength of thine own scars remain.
Thou the cross from dark to sun,
stretching boughs to wind and rain,
upholding all, withholding none.

Lord, on thee do I depend.
Thy limbs hold me, heal me, mend
all unbelieving doubts. And now
I do not break, I bend, I bend:
thou hast made of me a bough.

As thou depended from a tree
so depend I, Lord, on thee.
Of thy body made a part
I was blind, and now I see:
all life and love are because thou art.

Peter

Lord, I love you.
I have tried to feed your sheep.
Shepherds have a lonely job.

I have gone out searching for you
into the tumult of the midnight sky—
the swirling life of stars too many to count,
and have been deafened
by the rush of the wind.
And now you ask me to look within,
away from the vast and echoing sound without.

So I go down and in,
into the deepest, narrowest,
darkest, most brilliant
places of the heart.
I am battered by its beat
throbbing in my veins,
tension, release.
In the small space
between the beats,
the rhythm
yours, not mine,
yours is its time
to keep me here, in time,
in, deeper, deeper,
to the beating of my heart.

So I end where I began
and once again I start
to learn that my disgrace
is ripped, is torn apart,
and mended by your grace.

A Man from Phrygia, on Pentecost

Lord, I did not choose to be comforted.
I am not ready to bear the many things
you have yet to say: you said it yourself.
But you have sent me (against my will) your comforter
and what is comfort but an iron command?

I don't want to obey. I won't. Yes: I will.
Why must I interrupt my self-indulgent weakness
to respond to the austerity of your demand?
I must set my face sternly towards truth
as you turned toward Jerusalem, that all
obedience should be shown us and accomplished.
Your way to truth is hard, is dark, is pain.
You have shown me the way, O Lord, but I
am not prepared to bear your comfort.
And yet, unwilling, unready, recalcitrant,
I receive the flaming thrust that you have sent,
and voices speaking as in my own tongue,
and nothing will ever be the same again.

Barnabas, Travelling to Antioch

The road is long, my friend,
and not smooth. We expected
the dark forest, the thorns,
and unsuspected pitfalls.
We even knew that some
would turn away from us, toward
broader, easier roads. It hurt,
but did not surprise,
when they denied the way and placed traps
for the pilgrims. The sharp iron teeth
snapped shut, broke bone, made much blood.
And so we walked, dragging the brokenness.
Pain became a constant companion,
relieved only by laughter
and the breaking of bread.
In the darkness we sometimes hurt each other
and did not even know what we had done.

The road is long, my friend,
and the journey rough.
This harsh wood
prepared for each one on this path
grows heavy by afternoon.
There's not much rest.
We walk as strangers in this foreign land with no rest
and yet this uphill road leads to the light of home.
The night is far spent. The day is at hand.

Phoebe, Perhaps the Very First Deacon

Quoniam tu illuminas lucernam meam Domine:
Deus meus illumina tenebras meas.

There was fire in the bush when Moses first
spoke with God.
There was light too brilliant to be borne.
God covered the prophet's eyes with his hand.
And then in the darkness they talked.
Beyond sight, Moses heard
and listened to the Word.

But I am like a child at bedtime,
frightened of the dark,
crying out for a drink of water
that the door may open,
crying for water
but thirsty for light.

I must leave Egypt and follow the cloud,
for only in that place beyond the galaxies,
further than starfire and the blaze of suns,
only beyond all light, beyond all hope of human sight
will I see the source of all illumination
in the radiant glory of the Word.

But I am like a child in a strange house at night
groping through shadowy rooms

toward the sound of voices,
afraid to call and ask where the light can be found.

Further than any man can go alone
in the deepest, darkest reaches of the heart:
here the light is lit, the invisible light
by which alone we see.

Come light this tiny candle, Lord.
Give me a flame of understanding according to your
    Word.

Priscilla's Response to the Letter to the Hebrews

He is
the Word
Creator
he who shall be at the end
the glory
face of God
the cleanser, sin destroyer
the Visitor.

He is
greater than the angels
Son of the Father
the just ruler
the chosen one
the joyful.

He is
in Time
lower than the angels
perfect through suffering
our brother
the death destroyer.

and so
He is
our helper in temptation.

He is
our high priest
faithful in all things.

He is not
an angel, for he names them
and they worship him.

He will never
change or disappear
though he makes change
and will be at the end and beyond.

He is not
an angel, for he knows death

and when he died,
so did death.

He is not
untempted.

He is not
stubborn, as we are,
rebellious and tempting.

He is
our rest
and our Way of rest.

He is
the sword that cuts us open
exposing us to the Father.

He is
weak for our sakes

called to be our high priest.

He is
obedient unto death.

He is
the promiser
the keeper of the promise
the promise itself.

He is
the king of righteousness
the Prince of Peace
the blesser
and the blessing.

He does not
hear and refuse to believe.

He is not
indifferent to our weakness
unsympathetic to our pain
ungentle with our weakness.

He does not
choose himself but he is chosen.

He is not
a child like us, who must be
children before he can grow us up.
He will never
forget, nor be unfair, nor
impatient with our impatience.

He does not
collect from us one-tenth
but all.

He is not
so much the collector as
the collected.
He is not
the law, but the changer of the law.

He is
wholly different
the power of life which has no end.
He is
the one once sacrifice
high priest in the tent God
    pitched among us
the real pattern.

He is
the true testator
by the shedding of blood.

He pours
out his own blood to drown our sins.
　　He is
the end of the old sacrifices
the one forever sacrifice for sin
who with the sacrifice is perfecter.

　　He is
freedom from the law.

　　He is not
temporal power, or the old
covenant, which was in time.
　　He does not
pass on to others his work as priest
or offer daily sacrifice.
　　He is not
the shadow but the caster of shadow.
　　He does not
write his law on stone but in our hearts.

　　Not
the blood of goats or calves
　　but his own.

　　He is not
a copy of the original
repeating over and over

offering over and over what he
has offered once and forever.

He is not
the law.

He is
the way of truth, judge and fire
terrible
living God.

He is
who came
who will come.
He is
that which can be seen
from that which cannot be seen.
He
makes the world
condemns the world
redeems the world.

He is
the weak who is all strength
the dying who raises from the dead
who dies and rose
and sits at the right hand of God.

He is
the Son who suffered that we might become sons.

He is not
the possible but the impossible
leaving his own country

without knowing where he was going
and living with us as a
stranger in a strange land.

   He did not
think back to the country he had.
   He is not
Abraham but Isaac
not Isaac but the ram caught in
   the burning bush.

   He is not
obedient to the law but to God.

   He is
He who speaks.

   He is
the divine message
the earth shaker
destroying fire
destroying fear
unending
unchangeable
death dying
life raising.

   He is
the glory forever and ever.

      He is not
held in by any walls
but dies outside the gate
that we might follow him
leaving the temporal city
to share his shame
and so see the city
which is to come.

Amen   Amen   Amen

Mary Speaks: From Ephesus

Now that I have spent these years in this strange place
of luminous stone and golden light and dying gods,
now that I have listened to the wild music
of given-son, John, I begin to understand.

In the beginning I was confused and dazzled;
a plain girl, unused to angels.
Then there was the hard journey to Bethlehem,
and the desperate search for a place to stay,
my distended belly ripe and ready for deliverance.
In the dark of the cave, night air sweet with the moist
    breath
of domestic beasts, I laughed, despite my pains,
at their concern. Joseph feared that they would frighten
    me
with their anxious stampings and snortings,
but their anxiety was only for me, and not because of me.
One old cow, udder permanently drooping,
mooed so with my every contracting
that my birthing-cries could not be heard.
And so my baby came with pain and tears and much
    hilarity.

Afterwards, swaddled and clean, he was so small and
    tender
that I could not think beyond my present loving
to all this strange night pointed. The shepherds came
clumsily gruff and knelt, and brought their gifts,
and, later on, the kings; and all I knew was marvel.

His childhood was sheer joy to me. He was merry and
      loving,
moved swiftly from laughter to long, unchildlike silences.
The years before his death were bitter for me.
I did not understand, and sometimes thought that it
      was he
who had lost comprehension of the promise of his birth.

His death was horrible. But now I understand
that death was not his sacrifice, but birth.
It was not the cross which was his sacrifice.
It was his birth which must have been, for him,
most terrible of all. Think. If I were to be born
out of compassion, as one of the small wood-lice
in the door-sill of our hut, limit myself to the
      comprehension
of those small dark creatures, unable to know sea or sun
      or song
or John's bright words, to live and die thus utterly
      restricted,
it would be nothing, nothing to the radiant Word
coming to dwell, for man, in man's confined and cabined
      flesh.

This was the sacrifice, this ultimate gift of love.
I thought once that I loved. My love was hundredfold less
than his, than the love of the wood-lice is to mine,
and even this I do not know. For has he not, or will he not
come to the wood-lice as he came to man? Does he not
give his own self to the lowing cattle, the ear of corn,
the blazing sun, the clarion moon, the drop of rain?

His compassion is infinite, his sacrifice incomprehensible,
breaking through the darkness of our loving-lack.

Oh, my son, who was and is and will be, my night draws
    close.
Come, true light, which taketh away the sin of the world,
and bring me home. My hour is come. Amen.

Ephesus

They walked these self-same stones.
Mary was wilting, weary with the journey,
weary with the years and all that she
had understood and had not understood.
Obedient always, she deferred to John,
smiling a mother's smile at his great joy.
Chariots of gold raced through the godless streets;
Apollo and Diana had grown dim;
only the emperor was god.
They paused, perhaps, Mary and John,
at these same vacant gates
of the sad temple of forgotten gods,
and Mary smiled and turned and said,
"My son, the old gods have been lost."
And John replied, "Bring we now the new—"

And in his harrowing of a shadowed Hell
perhaps the old gods were redeemed as well,
and joyfully sing their praise to him
with cherubim and seraphim.

Mary Magdalene, Remembering:

All time is holy.
We move through the dark
following his footprints by touch.
He walked the lonesome valley.
His time is holy.

We will break bread together.
We will move through the dark.
He has gone away from us.
The wine is poured out.
We will eat broken bread.

That Friday was good.
We will move through the dark.
Death died on Friday.
The blood-stained cross bore hope.
His Friday is good.

We will hold hands
as we move through the dark.
Saturday he walked through hell,
making all things new.
We will hold hands.

This is the meaning
of our walk through the dark.
Love's light will lead us
through the stone at the tomb.
He is the meaning.

He called me by name
as I stood in the dark.
Suddenly I knew him.
He came. Then he left us,
he will come again.

"And Nicolas . . ."

And Nicolas a proselyte of Antioch, whom they set
before the apostles: and when they had prayed,
they laid their hands on them, and the word of God
increased.

—*Acts 6:5–7*

I don't understand, dear God.
Do you do it just to make us face
our abominable pride,
to prove to us what needs proving
over and over again:
that of ourselves we are nothing,
and then you take this nothing
that you have made from nothing
and use it to your own good purpose?

But why, Lord?
Surely there are people you could use
who are better than we,
either the old Israel or the new?
We don't flatter ourselves (do we?)
that we are the only ones you can choose
(circumcised or uncircumcised
always stiff-necked).

And then, it's not just your choice of a nation
or of those of us who are the dogs

who lick the crumbs from under your table,
but—O Lord, why, for instance, Abraham?
All those wiles and guiles which really weren't honest,
pretending before kings that his wife was his sister
because he was afraid? And we can't make believe
that Jacob's treatment and trickery of Esau
was anything but the kind of thing applauded
by the wily Romans who consider it smart
to step on your brother's hairy body
to get to the top of the ladder, angels or no.

And yet you chose those devious men.
To us it's irrational and arbitrary, the things you do
over and over again. You burst,
with cloud of your glory,
upon an arrogant tent-maker who would have
nailed you to the cross personally
if he had been on that hill top,
and failing that, delighted in seeing Christians
stoned to bloody, brutal death.
Could you not find even the ten just men
for whom to spare the city?

Why Abraham, why Jacob, why Saul, why me?
Come, then, Lord, as you have always done
to the unjust, the unjustified, the foolish.
Use us despite ourselves
whether we recognize you or not,
whether or not we see that the stumbling block

which you have laid before your people
is the cornerstone of the house.

You come to us, the hopelessly impenitent,
that to your purposes our rude wills may be bent.

UNCOLLECTED
POEMS

(circa 1966)

For Lent, 1966

It is my Lent to break my Lent,
    To eat when I would fast,
To know when slender strength is spent,
    Take shelter from the blast
When I would run with wind and rain,
    To sleep when I would watch.
It is my Lent to smile at pain
    But not ignore its touch.

It is my Lent to listen well
    When I would be alone,
To talk when I would rather dwell
    In silence, turn from none
Who call on me, to try to see
    That what is truly meant
Is not my choice. If Christ's I'd be
    It's thus I'll keep my Lent.

The Stripper

Someone has pushed me out onto the stage.
Pinned by the glare of spotlights, here I stand.
I am, for this kind of thing, long past the age,
Have had little experience of strip-teasing.
To unclothe myself before you I had not planned,
Having not found my person very pleasing.

But the orchestra has started; blatant music rises
With strings and drums and brasses from the pit.
The body I reveal holds no surprises,
No more nor less than any other strumpet.
I start my dance with little grace or wit
Prodded by glare of light and blare of trumpet.

One by one my garments I am shedding;
It helps that I am blinded by the light.
I once had daydreams of a proper wedding
And going purely to another being
Before I lost my way in this dark night.
Who is the audience my shame is seeing?

The veils, the skirt, the bodice off; I cast,
The undergarments, garter, shoe, and stocking.
The music prods me. Stop! It is too fast!
My heartbeat falters and my breath is spent.
I should not strip before you. It is shocking
Me if no one else. But I am Lent

From somewhere now the courage to continue
This ritual dance of nakedness and shame,
Revealing shrinking flesh and timid sinew.
I've done. I cannot take off any more.
What? You require my flesh, my eyes, my *name*?
I would not have come in by that stage door

If I had known this staggering demand.
I'm naked now. Oh, surely this is all!
Oh, God: it hurts! Could you have had it planned,
This act beyond the usual stripper's turn?
Blind now, and deaf; now bone and muscle fall:
There is a coal upon my tongue. I burn.

It is all gone. I'm naught. The stage is bare,
The music stilled. Through silence comes your voice
To fill the void with beauty everywhere.
Stripped wholly in this strange and painful fashion
The bones that you have broken now rejoice,
Knit up and clothed again by your compassion.

The Baptism of Easter, 1966

Back in those times still lost in time
Within the memory of the dinosaur
When slowly we began to climb
From fish to reptile, beast, and bird,
When fire and smoke and flame could roar
And song from tree and cave was heard:

Back in those times of man not man,
Of man not separate from beast,
Pursued by beast I turned and ran
And, stumbling, into water fell,
Plunged under; breathing almost ceased.
Half drowned, I surfaced and could tell

For the first time in history
That I, now man, had nearly died;
I felt the power of mystery:
Awareness shocked: I knew, I knew:
Shed my first tears and knew I cried.
Mortality had broken through

The endless life of innocence:
For instinct understands no death.
Terror, new born, became immense,
For when I knew that I was I
I felt the strain of every breath,
That heart would cease and man would die:

Would die to water, fire, or earth,
Would turn to dust, return to air.
The river gave a shocking birth
To questions never asked before.
The pain of being thus aware
Became the burden that I bore.

What pain to know! Yet not to know
Compounds with fear the initial sin.
Plunge me beneath the water's flow
And bring me forth, reborn, to hear
The light, to see the Word within
My heart! The end of time draws near:

So am I born, not born of blood
Or will of flesh or will of man,
But spirit, fire, and the wild flood
That wakens and renews the clay;
The living waters are the span
That bears the weight of night and day.

Small Galaxy

I am fashioned as a galaxy,
Not as a solid substance but a mesh
Of atoms in their rich complexity
Forming the pattern of my bone and flesh.
Small solar systems are my eyes.
Muscle and sinew are composed of air.
Like comets flashing through the evening skies
My blood runs, ordered, arrogant, and fair.

Ten lifetimes distant is the nearest star,
And yet within my body, firm as wood,
Proton and electron separate are.
Bone is more fluid than my coursing blood.
What plan had God, so strict and so impassioned
When he an island universe my body fashioned?

For Pentecost, 1966 (1)

Why, at this time of coming of your Spirit,
Do I keep thinking of that Saturday
Before you rose, your kingdom to inherit?
Why am I smothered in the tomb's dark closing
So that the horror when you went away
(And no one dreamed of dayspring and your rising)
Reeks in my nose with gravecloth stench? Today
When I should see the flaming of the dove
Why do I hear the dirge of hopeless mourning,
Of empty tears to cry the death of Love?
Must all love have its silent Saturday?
There is a night between each brilliant morning.
I must walk through it, since you paved the way.

Lines After Hymn 456

My God, I love Thee, not because
I love of my own choice,
Nor could I of myself respond
To thine embodied voice;
My love could only come from Thee
To my heart's darkest place,
And darkness had to blind my mind
Before I saw Thy face.

I sought Thee out of my own will,
But there love cannot dwell;
And seeking love, demanding love,
I stumbled, and I fell.
And there, my Lord, thou sent'st me love
To make my heart aflame;
Now, like the Phoenix, love is risen,
Is hallowed by Thy name.

I cannot love Thee, God, because
Thou first gave love to me,
Or for Thy life, or for Thy death,
And sweat of agony:
Of my own will I cannot love
The shining of Thy face,
But only through the radiant
Unexpectedness of Grace.

"My sins, I fear, dear Lord, lack glamour"

My sins, I fear, dear Lord, lack glamour.
   I'll never make a thief.
In the market place's lustful clamour
   I do not seek relief.

I'm not a greedy tax collector,
   I pay my tax instead.
I'm neither killer nor draft defector;
   I earn my daily bread.

Euphoria in Needle Park
   Has never been temptation.
I go to bed when it is dark.
   My acts of contemplation

Are apt to be on household chores
   And bringing up the baby.
I'm of the company of bores
   Who're worth salvation—maybe.

The church's doors are open wide
   As they should always be
To anyone who'll go inside—
   Except for those like me.

Adultery would help me in,
   Or any strange perversion.

Masses of money would begin
    To put the greedy spurs on

The exquisite unfriendly church
    Where mass media are able
To supercede the Mass, and perch
    Upon the Holy Table.

If I could couch my current quest
    In language fine and formal,
I'd ask that simple souls be blest:
    Salvation for the normal.

Intention for Mass: Watts, Viet Nam, Johannesburg . . .

This is my body which is given for you . . .
Without exception. There is not a one
For whom he did not die. And I, and you
Must die in the same way. What he's begun
Must be continued daily by us all
Without exception: for the sinned against
We die no more than for our sinning race.
We, sinning, die by his blood cleansed;
He dies and lives within us by his grace
    For lynchers, lynched, for blind men in the night
    He died, and death then gives to us our sight.

"I am become like a pelican . . ."

I am become like a pelican in the wilderness. . . .
For I have eaten ashes as it were bread,
and mingled my drink with weeping. . . .
But thou, O LORD, shalt endure for ever.

—Psalm 102:6, 9, 12

God is dead? Well, of course God is dead!
Where have you been? Did you not see the dark
Cover the hill and strike against the cross?
We killed him then two thousand years ago
And once was not enough. We kill him now
In each denial, each unloving act.
Daily we kill him, trampling on his name,
Spitting on his word. And we are told,
And rightly, that he died between two thieves
And not two candles shining on an altar.
And yet there, too, perhaps most terribly,
He's crucified each day by priest and those
Who take him, unaware of all the clouds
Of witnesses encompassing them in song
And prayer, who kneel there coldly unaware
Of those who suffer in the adjoining pew.
We do not understand his feast; we live
Again his crucifixion, but forget,
Each time we crucify him there again
Between those candles whose bright flame is lost
To darkened eyes, that when he died for us

After three days he rose, and still for us.
We kill him, but we cannot keep his light
From blazing forth in flame for every one
Who fouls his word and calls him dead and cries
In loneliness because his name is lost.

And yet, receiving now my heart's true food
I feel his light rush coursing through my blood.
Nourished by his spilled wine and broken bread,
I know that my Redeemer is not dead.

UNCOLLECTED

POEMS

(circa 1998)

Sonnet 1

Your place is empty, empty in the night
When I reach out with hand or foot to touch
Your living flesh, the warmth that offers such
An affirmation, oh, it is not right
The bed is empty, made for two, not one.
The reflex does not die, to touch, to reach,
To find. I think it will be never done,
And I am glad of that. It seems that each
Of us find our own answers in this grief.
I know you have been here. You have been here.
The empty place is full of deep relief
Because it still is yours and still is dear.
But oh! That my dear love were in my bed
And my life flesh to your live flesh still wed.

Sonnet 2

How long your closet held a whiff of you,
Long after hangers hung austere and bare.
I would walk in and suddenly the true
Sharp sweet sweat scent controlled the air
And life was in that small still living breath.
Where are you? Since so much of you is here,
Your unique odour quite ignoring death.
My hands reach out to touch, to hold what's dear
And vital in my longing empty arms.
But other clothes fill up the space, your space,
And scent on scent send out strange false alarms.
Not of your odour there is not a trace.
But something unexpected still breaks through
The goneness to the presentness of you.

Sonnet 3

This, too, is passion, the so gentle touch
Of fingertip to wrist, to shoulder, face.
More would cause pain, and oh I would not such
Anguish awake, I sit here in my place
Beside this strange white bed, with IV poles
Holding snaked lines that feed into your arms.
A limbo, this, a waiting room for souls
Ready to leave the flesh with all its charms—
And I am still in thrall to human love,
To tough, to whisper, bring from you a smile.
Passion remains. What am I thinking of?
How can I let it go? Hold on a while.
But oh, my love, must I now love you so
That my love's passion has to let you go?

Sonnet 4

The prince is turned to dragon, beast, or toad,
And I in deep enchanted sleep seem dead.
Who has the key, the door, the hidden road?
Whose kiss will rouse the princess from the bed,
Free the young prince from the unnatural spell
That keeps his body in its bitter thrall?
Both need the kiss, the lad, the lass as well,
So eyes may open, shrunken limbs grow tall.
You kissed me, love, and woke me from my sleep.
My lips met yours, and thus I kissed you, too.
Spells were undone, and we with joy did weep.
It was the kiss that made the story true.
Look! Watch the evil spell break into shards,
The story is the light beyond the words.

Sonnet 5

Child and old woman, here again I sit,
Adolescent, mother, yet I'm still
Presiding at the table, candles lit,
Widow and wife I am. The plates I fill
With food set out at places freshly laid
Are honoring with love each coming guest.
How many are the meals that I have made
Night after night, nor can find one the best?
I'll keep the laughter and the sad shed tears,
Would give none up; one lost would make me less.
Add all in all, the ecstasies, the fears.
Together they redeem, restore, redress.
I light the candles, bless the food, and you
Who grace the table make the myth come true.

Sonnet 6

In the hotel room the phone is there.
Thoughtless, I walk towards it, start to dial.
pause, fingers now uncertain. Where oh where
is your new number? Will it in a while
Be given to me? And will I ever call,
"Darling, I'm safely here. Love, it is I."?
There is no number now, not one at all
To reach beyond your death. I cannot cry
My love across the line to where you are.
I do not know! My love, I do not know
If you're still near or have gone very far.
I cannot use the phone. The answer's. No.
Where did death take you that the phone
Is useless and I hear my voice alone?

Sonnet 7

"It is not good for man to be alone," said God.
So God made two to be forever one,
And failed. Formed from dust and lowly sod
The two could not leave well enough alone.
They turned from God and ate forbidden fruit,
So God exiled them from their birthright home.
They knew each other, then. The point is moot.
Lost, hungry, they were forced to roam
The world of spirit more than that of earth.
They knew each other, then, the pain of love
That made two one, and was the cause of birth.
How strangely wise of God to make them move.
Only by breaking and mending can we be
The unique one, by God's wild love set free.

Sonnet 8

Did we know fear when we were born?
Moving from small safety (safety's always
small), from our known comforts roughly torn
Into the blinding light of noisy hallways.
Was it like death? our old world left behind,
Air knifing unused lungs, light rough
Against our womb-protected eyes, still blind.
In that warm wet place was it not enough?
Yet in this new life, we've been satisfied.
So must you leave me now, from life released?
Your body's cold. I know that it has died.
Is death another birth? Is death deceased?
All that I know of you goes back to earth.
I do not know if this is death or birth.

Sonnet 9

Resurrection's not resuscitation.
What, in heaven's name, do we expect?
I'm satisfied with no one's explanation
Which seem to me more fancy than correct.
I know that hour beloved body's gone
And heaven's not pie in some ethereal sky.
It's you I want, familiar flesh and bone.
But my flesh, too, is mortal. I will die.
So what, then, do I hope from resurrection?
I hope beyond my wildest hope unseen
That there will still be some aware connection
'Twixt what we will be and 'twixt what we've been,
And you and I and all we love will meet
When Love has won, and we're at last complete.

Sonnet 10

Don't tell me that his pain is over now.
Don't tell me cancer is a good God's will.
Don't talk about the Great Prime Mover, how
He knows all things, controls the future still.
Give me God who makes his creatures free
To play the story to a glorious finish,
Whose power is in relinquishing power, so we
May grow in love. Oh, let his power diminish
As he comes in to us with all our pain,
Who shows magnificence upon a cross,
Who o'er a groaning universe does reign
Until love triumphs over every loss.
Only this God is strong enough to say
"I love you," and so throw all power away.

Sonnet 11

God! The world is so big, our tiny lives so small,
How can we believe that our little love matters?
Death has torn all I care for to terrible tatters.
Did our love matter? Oh, God, does it matter at all?
Countless galaxies swirl in the alien spaces,
Great furnaces of raging nuclear power
Against whose blasts the comets swiftly shower
Reflecting heaven on our human faces.
Life and death are hardly held apart
And yet this one death's impact is so great
The breathing of the universe must wait
Upon the ceasing of this single heart.
Dear love, if what I feel now is not true,
God never was, not God, not I, not you.

Sonnet 12

I suppose they could have called us counter-culture.
You, an actor on the stage, and I
Writing novels, looking towards a future
Where we'd take off and care free, fly.
Care free? No, life's richer far than that,
But work we did, and children had, and grew
Through joy and pain, not even knowing what
Was best or worst. Tears, not a few,
Balanced our lives, you on the stage,
Movies, TV, while I worked with my pen,
Adding pages to my books, each page
Both sweat and joy. We loved. We loved. And then—
You're gone. And though ye leave me not bereft
Nothing has been the same since you have left.

Sonnet 13

O God! You ask the deepest darkest things.
You blind with light more frightening than dark.
You tell me: Fly! And then you give no wings.
Your sharp sword pierces as it hits the mark.
You gave me love as human as the earth
And earth to earth you've gone as all must go.
So we are torn apart 'twixt tears and mirth
And where your *you* has gone I do not know.
Oh, God! Your loneliness came into flesh.
You taught us love as you let all love go,
And with your life our lives are deep enmeshed.
We know you as we know we do not know.
Oh, God! You ask us all to be like you,
And what you love will truly be made new.

Sonnet 14

You hurt me, so I turned away and wept.
Did I hurt you, and were you slapping back?
It hurt. But we curled up like spoons and slept
And of our salty tears we kept no track.
Why do we lose each other? Where are you?
I've forgotten who you are, you see,
And in your anger have you lost me, too?
Can we be found again? Do you know me?
Now in each other we'll find someone new
And fall in love again. We can't return
To who we were. I'm me, my dear, you're you.
From who we were to who we are we'll learn
And oh, my dark, our love is more by far
Because our hurts have made us who we are.

Iona, 1

This land is holy:
the sheep and the lambs
the abbeys destroyed
in the name of God
the remains of stone huts
for God-seeking hermits
the prayers of the nuns
still lingering like fog
despite rape and the fire
the sound of their voices
singing the praises
of God and the morning
the water for washing
the pots for the porridge
the fishermen's nets
and the sunset through raindrops.
When we weren't looking
holiness broke through
bright as a rainbow.

The Donkey

I recognize angels.
Donkey's can see what mortals fail to recognize.
He beat me, did Balaam,
beat me to move on,
for he was blind and did not see
the angel barring our path.
I saw.
Angels mean business.
I stopped.

Go, the angel said. Go quickly.
You are bearing holiness.
I moved gently, not to jolt the woman
who carried within her
all light and life and love
waiting to be born.
Go, the angel said. It is time.

Again I saw angels.
Their wings were held high over my burden,
the weary man if light sitting on my back,
staring at the shadow of a cross.
We were covered in darkness.
People tossed palm branches before us.
"Go," the angels said. "Go."
They were not like the other angels.
Their wings drooped, though they tried
to hold them high. "Go," the angels said,

"into the darkness."
"Go," the angels said,
"through the darkness into the light."

And we did go.

"The page is torn from a journal—
though not mine—"

The page is torn from a journal—though not mine—
The journal of the poet. Purple shade
Smudges the spill of light from the late day sun.
The ink will run if I cannot remember
To keep the darkness new—so easily forgot.
The night provides more light than blatant day.
What can I write that keeps that morning fresh
That hid the young cat in the row of wheat?

The reaper lacks the eyes to hold him back;
Unseeing, his sharp blade carves its damning cut
That kills without a conscious, caring thought.
He does not hear the harsh cry of the cat;
It shouts against this unexpected death,
And spurting blood, and life gone like the wind.

80

Now that I've gone beyond the middle middle
I wrote at forty seven
feeling at last I'd got there,
maturity, I mean,
borne children
watched one barely survive death one winter weekend
fought with my husband and made up
wept and laughed, grieved and let go—
how long and young ago was that
Now that I've gone beyond the Bible's life span
been warned by the psalmist, dour as Ecclesiastes
that everything is bleak and dark
I rejoice in family, friends, flowers
dance at my granddaughter's wedding
weep at another marriage broken
laugh as we sit twelve at a table meant for eight
Now that I've twice (almost)
gone beyond the middle middle
I smile at statistics I could never comprehend
I see death's shadow stretch its barren trees
showing structure and surprising beauty,
promising that the journey does not end.
Perhaps now—forgetting fat maturity—
I'm ready to let go
into the questioning child
who has always understood
that love is endless
numbers do not threaten
and Yes! Each day is a new challenge
a new birth.

Editor's Note

The nature of this collection necessitated a number of editorial decisions regarding the order and version of the poems included. In most instances, we included the earliest version of a poem published. One exception to this is the "Three Songs of Mary." Although *"O Sapientia"* and *"O Simplicitas"* were first published in *The Weather of the Heart,* we publish them here under *A Cry Like a Bell* so they can remain with *"O Oriens,"* a poem added later to complete the series. Also, in a number of cases, a poem published in *The Irrational Season* was later updated for publication in *A Cry Like a Bell* or *The Weather of the Heart.* In those cases, we deferred to the later version of a poem so we might include the version that first appeared in a full-length book of poetry. This collection also includes twenty-seven poems that had not been collected previously. Finally, some minor edits were made to conform poems to the editorial style of this collection.

Reader's Guide

by Lindsay Lackey

For me, Madeleine L'Engle has long been an icon.

I have been reading her work since I was a child, beginning, as so many do, with *A Wrinkle in Time* and *A Ring of Endless Light,* then later finding my way slowly, purposefully, through her fiction for children and adults. From there I journeyed into her spiritual writings, her essays and speeches, before finally discovering her poetry.

With her fiction, Madeleine taught me not only to ask questions, but also to lean into mystery. Through her nonfiction, I discovered my ability to sit with discomfort and began to acknowledge the darkness in my own soul. But it was here, in *The Ordering of Love,* where I first encountered Madeleine's poetry as a collection—and in it, I believe I have met a Madeleine I have never seen before.

In Luci Shaw's introduction to the 2005 edition of *The Ordering of Love,* she writes, "In a way distinct from her novels and nonfiction prose, these individual poems introduce Madeleine to us like brief but intimate conversations with her. We can interact with her as we would with a friend. . . ."

I found a delightful truth in Luci's words as I read these poems for the first time. Here, I met a Madeleine who was rooted in her own time, yet fully relevant to my own. To see her most intimate thoughts expressed in moments of such dailiness, such as in "Lines Scribbled on an Envelope While Riding the 104 Broadway Bus," humanized the icon of the Madeleine I have known for so long.

Of course, I've always known her to be a human—her writing is raw and passionate in a way that makes her humanity undeniable. But the inherent immediacy of her poetry, the intimacy of it, reminded me that she was not, as I have come to call her, St. Madeleine—or at least not *just* St. Madeleine. She was a woman as enfleshed as I am. A woman who loved and grieved, who knew the blood and pain of childbirth, who felt the flash of anger at a rude stranger and the ache of despair over the suffering of an unknown child.

Reading Madeleine L'Engle is, for me, always a moment of connection. She has taught me to better connect with the world around me, with God, with myself. But here I was given the gift of connecting with Madeleine, the woman, anew. She became not only a beloved teacher or storyteller or spiritual icon but also, as Luci Shaw said, a friend.

As Madeleine herself says, *Lord God! The icon's here, alive and free.*

From *Lines Scribbled on an Envelope* (1969)

1. Choose one of the first five poems in this section and read it again. Which poem did you choose? What lines struck you as you read? What images stood out? Why?

2. Take some time to more closely analyze the poem you've chosen. What is the poem's structure? How does L'Engle use meter and rhyme? How does the rhythm of this poem enhance its meaning? Does this poem read differently to you when read aloud than it does when read silently?

3. How does the poem you've chosen examine love? Why do you think you were drawn to this particular message of love?

4. L'Engle's poetry embraces the mythological (e.g., "Medusa,"

"The Unicorn"), her contemporary world ("For Dana: 4th November," "From St. Luke's Hospital [I]"), and multiple explorations of spirituality ("Testament," "Fire by Fire," "Moses"). Reading this collection of her poetry from 1969 feels almost like having a conversation with the author about story, about life, faith, and, of course, love. What aspects of this "conversation" resonate most deeply with you? What poems stand out and why?

5. Pick a favorite poem from this section and, as if it really were a conversation, write your response. You can write in verse— perhaps mimicking the author's style—or in simple prose. What does this poem mean to you? What questions do you have for L'Engle? How does this poem speak to your faith, understanding, or worldview? How does this poem challenge you?

From *The Irrational Season* (1977)

1. What differences in style and tone do you see between this collection and the first? In what ways has time changed or informed the poet's voice, form, or approach? What topics appear to have grown in importance between these two poetic eras in her life? What themes are new in this collection?

2. How does L'Engle acknowledge pain, suffering, and darkness in these poems? Does one stand out to you in particular? How, if at all, does she balance her exploration of these themes with love and light?

3. The poem "Boarding school: someone cried jubilantly" details L'Engle's memories of her father's death. How does the imagery she uses reflect her feelings of loss? What images come to mind when you think of losses you have suffered? In what ways do you relate to this poem?

4. How does L'Engle's use of rhyme and meter enrich her ex-

amination of a theme? Select one of her rhyming poems from this section and consider how her choice to rhyme shapes the poetry. What moments become surprising or joyful because of her language?

5. Several pieces in this collection are Christmas poems. Which Christmas poem is your favorite? Why? What themes seem, at first glance, unrelated to the typical view of Christmas? Do any of her images or phrases particularly surprise or move you? Why?

From *The Weather of the Heart* (1978)

1. Compare the different "To a Long Loved Love" poems in this section. What aspects of love does she examine in each? Why do you think L'Engle chose to write these poems as sonnets?

2. Consider the short poem "Epiphany." What strikes you about this poem? Why do you think it is called "Epiphany"?

3. Several poems here are explorations of biblical characters. How do these poems enrich or challenge your own understanding of the characters portrayed?

4. L'Engle writes about pain, about loss, about hope and darkness and the birth of children. How do each of these poems reflect her overall theme of love and order?

5. Look again at the poem "Love Letter." Have you ever wanted to write a letter to God? Do you have questions that seem to be reflected in L'Engle's words? Have you ever hated God? How do you express your anger toward God?

From *A Cry Like a Bell* (1987)

1. This collection of poetry was published nearly a decade after her last. What differences in theme or style do you notice in

this collection compared to the earlier three? What topics seem to have gained importance to her here?

2. The majority of poems in this section are biblically based. In what ways does L'Engle's exploration of biblical characters relate to contemporary life? How do her words humanize these characters for you?

3. Select one of the poems in this section. Read the biblical story related to your choice. (For example, if you chose "Thomas: After Seeing the Wounds," read John 20:24–29.) How does the poem change your understanding of the scriptural account? How does the tone of the poem differ from the tone in the Bible passage? What structure does L'Engle use for the poem, and how does that shape its narrative?

Uncollected Poems (circa 1966 and circa 1998)

1. How do the poems from this first era differ from her later poetry? What changes do you see in the author's poetry over time? Do you find yourself connecting most with poems from a particular era of her life? Why or why not?

2. Why do you think L'Engle so often chose to write in the sonnet form? In what ways do you think sonnets are restricting? In what ways are they freeing?

3. What themes in her sonnets resonate most with you? Why?

4. Choose one of the poems from these sections and spend some time with it. What is it about? What theme is she exploring? In what form is the poem written? Highlight some of the imagery that is most striking. What turns surprise you? How does the poem challenge you? What draws you to this particular piece?

Index of Titles

Index of First Lines

ABOUT THE AUTHOR

MADELEINE L'ENGLE was the author of more than fifty
books for all ages, including *A Wrinkle in Time* and *A Swiftly
Tilting Planet*. Other popular L'Engle books include *Walking on
Water, The Rock That Is Higher,* and *Penguins and Golden Calves.*

ABOUT THE TYPE

This book was set in Garamond, a typeface originally designed by the Parisian type cutter Claude Garamond (c. 1500–61). This version of Garamond was modeled on a 1592 specimen sheet from the Egenolff-Berner foundry, which was produced from types assumed to have been brought to Frankfurt by the punch cutter Jacques Sabon (c. 1520–80).

Claude Garamond's distinguished romans and italics first appeared in *Opera Ciceronis* in 1543–44. The Garamond types are clear, open, and elegant.